KETOGENIC AIR FRYER
COOKBOOK FOR BEGINNERS

Foolproof Air Fryer Recipes
for Busy People on Keto Diet

Jessica Davis

CONTENTS

Brunch recipes 56

Beef and Lamb Recipes 76

Meatless Recipes...154

Desserts 168

Conclusion 177

INTRODUCTION

The recipes in this book are meant to be straightforward and delicious while also being healthy. My goal is for you to be able to get a healthy meal on the table in about 30 minutes or less without having to spend a ton of time or money at the grocery store.

You will find some recipes to be longer than an hour which is mostly related to their refrigeration time, and this is fine for a good turnout.

On the other hand, every recipe in this book can be prepared quickly from readily available ingredients at the grocery store. Do a read through the methods and make sure to understand the processes before you start cooking. It will make you enjoy the cooking process better.

WHAT IS THE KETO DIET?

It is merely a less or no carb form of eating where starchy and high carb foods are swapped for other ingredients; these low carb foods tend to yield better results.

A high carb diet is one that has 20% and more of complex carbohydrates in its content. Digestion is more difficult with such foods as the body has to struggle to break the complex substances into smaller units. In the end, your body holds up food longer than necessary in the body.

High carb diets are major contributors to weight gain and likely problems as well as sugar causing diseases like diabetes. Going ketogenic is a sure way to prevent these health problems, and they come with a feel-good factor.

Top 5 Ketogenic Diet Benefits.

1. Weight Loss

You will mainly not be feeding on starchy or complex carb foods when dieting, so the body naturally can break down foods like protein and fat quickly.

Starchy foods do not digest well and fast. They stay in the body for longer yielding to bloating and weight gain.

2. Heart Health Improvement

When dieting right on a ketogenic diet, that is, not falling onto high levels of bad fat, the amount of bad cholesterol in the body reduces significantly. Good cholesterol then aids the heart in functioning just right.

3. Aids with brain functioning

The high protein content in the keto diet offers neuroprotective benefits to the brain which goes to prevent brain diseases and sleeping disorders. A dedicated keto lifestyle strengthens the brain's muscles over time which leads to cognitive functioning and alertness.

4. A suppressed appetite

Sugar is known to make you hungrier faster which results in easy weight gains from very frequent feeding. On the keto diet, the body feeds on protein and good fat which have the tendencies of filling the stomach up for a long while. A consistent ketosis diet gradually allows you to eat smaller amounts of food hence a significant weight loss.

5. Improves women health

Sounds fantastic and this is true. A high carb diet can affect those with the polycystic ovarian syndrome (PCOS) negatively which is a disorder that causes enlarged ovaries with cysts.

Eating lots of vegetables and more protein allows the hormones to regulate blood glucose levels which normalizes PCOS to will enable the body to ovulate on time, hence fertility.

What can you eat while you're on a Keto diet?

You are meant to cut down on carbs when on a keto diet and eat more proteins, however in moderation. Ketosis foods could seem very light in the beginning, and you may be tempted to munch on something more substantial which often contains carbs. Make sure to remove all of such temptations to make your dieting successful. Some foods to keep are:

- **Vegetables with no starch** – These include a lot of green vegetables than root ones. These foods have little to no carb contents in them and are the safest options to eat. Some types are asparagus, leafy greens, broccoli, radishes, zucchinis, and lots of avocados.

- **Grass-fed meats** – Beef, lamb, pork derived from animals that fed only on grass keeps their meat healthy. Meats mainly do not contain any carbs making it very safe to add to your meals. These types of meat are also less fatty and have the right amounts of protein for the perfect dieting needs.

- **Fish and seafood** – Depending on what name suits you right, these are animals that grow in the sea which feed on protein. They have zero amount of carbs making them a run to option. Most often, people may be uncomfortable with the smell of seafood hence it is best to go for a recipe that has good flavoring to get these smells off. This book shares excellent recipes for this purpose.

- **Healthy fats** – It is not wrong to have fatty foods on a keto diet, but the ones with bad fats like fried foods is not a great idea. Aim for seafood, cheese, creams, fatty fish, nuts like hazelnuts, pecans, walnuts, pine nuts, brazil nuts, and seeds like sesame seeds, pumpkin seeds, and flaxseeds which have healthy fats and do not lead to weight gain and its accompanying problems. Use olive oil mostly for frying or stewing as it contains very little fat.

Also, make sure not to use low-fat creams as they often contain high carb contents to replace the fat content.

What you can't eat while you're on a keto diet?

Make sure to eat these kinds of foods in limited or no quantities.

- **Fruits** – They are very high in sugars, stay away from them except avocados. Eat lots of avocados.

- **Root vegetables** – Like potatoes, cabbages, carrots, artichokes, fennel bulbs, these have higher contents of carbs. You can have them, but they should be in small quantities.

- **Tubers and Grains** – These are very high in starch and complex carbs. Block them out of your keto diet.

- **Wines, Sweet Drinks, and Sweets** – Wines can be used for cooking but in minimal quantities. Sweet drinks, however, should be blocked as the sugar in them is a high carb ingredient.

WHAT IS AN AIR FRYER?

We all want to eat, and the first thing we do is to draw out a Whole Meal plan because we are aiming at cutting down the fats, which is good, but we forget about the cooking process.

The Air Fryer is modern cooking equipment that cooks food with little to no fat using a hot air blowing technique. It comes with a fryer basket were food placed and set to cook under hot air to cook it faster than an oven and crispier.

This method of cooking has proven to be one of the healthiest forms of cooking in existence and in combination with the keto recipes that we share, the goal to live healthier is made easier.

Seven Benefits of the Air Fryer

The benefits of this cooking device are in a wide range, and I will share the most important ones.

Time-Saving

For busy moms, hungry girls, and impatient cooks, this is the device to go for. It gets foods ready in just a few minutes while yielding fantastic results.

Weight Watching

Just because it cooks with no to little fat, your chances of adding on more weight can be controlled easily.

Easy to Use

You don't have to deal with several buttons to get it working. The cooking settings are very straightforward to apply. With the recipe in hand, select the temperature and time level, and you're good to go.

Easy to Clean

Who loves cleaning devices with complicated designs? Not me! The Air Fryer comes with a good set up that allows you to clean the fryer basket and food trapper very easily. Just wash them with wipes and dry with a napkin. That easy!

Multiple Cooking Options

You can bake, fry, roast, sauté, and grill with the Air Fryer and guess what you can choose not to oil your food when doing any of these. Meaning, you will not have to fill your kitchen with the different appliances to cook variety.

Space Saver

Many Air Fryers are designed to save space. They can fit in almost every area and are light to move around. You can have it set on the dinner table and dish food out from it onto the family's plates.

Energy Saving

They do not heat spaces and use lesser electricity than an electric oven. If you're not up for the heat in summer, this is one that will serve you well.

How to Use an Air Fryer?

In 5 to 6 steps you should be able to use an air fryer for the best result and long-lasting use.

Shake the fryer basket once or twice when making smaller foods like croquettes, wings, and meatballs. It ensures that the food is well cooked.

Never overcrowd the fryer basket when cooking. Work in batches for optimum results.

If there's a need to oil your foods, **always** go for cooking sprays as they are lighter and will not clog the holes of the fryer basket or make them greasy.

When cooking foods that have been marinated for a while, **pat them dry** before placing them in the fryer basket else the liquid will drop into the residue trapper and create the other mess.

Use heatproof bowls when there's a need to use a container in the air fryer.

Just **clean** the air fryer with a wet napkin or soak the fryer basket in soapy water before scrubbing or washing in the dishwasher.

Is an Air Fryer Good for a Keto Diet?

Yes and yes! It is one of the best for it. You can cook all kinds of vegetables and meats in the Air Fryer, and they will turn out excellently. Its use of less to no fat makes it all the better to use when making keto foods leaving out the trouble of taking in more fats.

However, sauces and highly liquid dishes may not be made in the Air Fryer because of the design of the fryer basket which has holes in it. You are better off making dryer or solid foods with it or else prepare saucy foods in a heatproof dish placed in the fryer basket. I added some recipes to show you how to do this.

Now, onto the recipes, have a great time making and **enjoying these tasty dishes**.

SNACKS AND APPETIZERS

Tasty Chicken Nuggets

Total Time: 1 hr 25 min | **Serves**: 4 | **Per serving**: Cal 523; Net Carbs 6.9g; Fat 46.1g; Protein 46.9g

Ingredients

2 chicken breasts, skin and bones removed
2 tbsp paprika
2 cups coconut milk
2 eggs
4 tsp onion powder

1 ½ tsp garlic powder
Salt and black pepper to taste
2 cups almond flour
2 cups pork rinds, crushed

Directions

Cut the chicken into 1-inch chunks. In a small bowl, add the paprika, onion powder, garlic powder, salt, pepper, almond flour, and pork rinds. Mix well.

In another bowl, crack the eggs, add the coconut milk and beat them together.

Prepare a tray aside. Dip each chicken chunk in the egg mixture, place on the tray, and refrigerate for 1 hour. Preheat the Air Fryer to 370°F.

After 1 hour, remove the chicken and roll each chunk in the pork rind mixture.

Open the Air Fryer and place the crusted chicken in the fryer basket. Spray with cooking spray. Slide in the fryer basket and cook for 4 minutes.

Pull out the fryer basket, flip the chicken chunks, spray with cooking spray, and cook further for 4 minutes. Prepare a wire rack and remove the chicken onto it once ready.

Serve the nuggets with a tomato dipping sauce or sugar-free ketchup. Yum!

Button Mushrooms with Cheese

Total Time: 55 min | **Serves**: 4 | **Per serving**: Cal 378; Net Carbs 7.3g; Fat 20.4g; Protein 38g

Ingredients

1 lb small button mushrooms, well cleaned
2 cups pork rinds, crushed
2 eggs, beaten
Salt and black pepper to taste

2 cups Parmigiano Reggiano cheese, grated

Directions

Preheat the Air Fryer to 360°F.

Pour the pork rinds in a bowl, add the salt and pepper and mix well.

Pour the cheese in a separate bowl and set aside. Dip each mushroom in the eggs, then in the pork rinds, and then in the cheese. Slide out the fryer basket and add 6 to 10 mushrooms to it.

Close the Air Fryer and cook them for 20 minutes. Once ready, remove to a serving plate and repeat the cooking process for the remaining mushrooms.

Lemon-Flavored Cupcakes

Total Time: 22 min | **Serves**: 5 | **Per serving**: Cal 412; Net Carbs 2g; Fat 25g; Protein 4.6g

Ingredients

Lemon frosting:

1 cup unsweetened natural yogurt   1 tbsp lemon zest
Swerve sweetener to taste   7 oz cream cheese
1 lemon, juiced

Cupcakes:

2 lemons, quartered   1 tsp vanilla extract
½ cup almond flour + extra for basing   2 eggs
¼ tsp salt   ½ cup butter, softened
2 tbsp swerve sweetener   2 tbsp coconut milk
1 tsp baking powder

Directions

Start with the frosting: in a bowl, add the yogurt and cream cheese. Mix using a fork until smooth. Add the lemon juice and zest. Mix well. Gradually add the sweetener to your taste while stirring until smooth. Make sure the frost is not runny. Set aside.

To make the cupcakes, place the lemon quarters in a food processor and process it until pureed. Add the almond meal, baking powder, softened butter, coconut milk, eggs, vanilla extract, swerve sweetener, and salt. Process again until smooth.

Preheat the Air Fryer to 400°F. Flour the bottom of 10 cupcake cases and spoon the batter into the cases ¾ way up. Place in the Air Fryer and bake them for 7 minutes. Once ready, remove them and let them cool. Design the cupcakes with the frosting.

Awesome Vegetable Croquettes

Total Time: 95 min | **Serves**: 4 | **Per serving**: Cal 224; Net Carbs 8.6g; Fat 14.2g; Protein 10.3g

Ingredients

1 ½ cups pork rinds, crushed
1 lb turnips
2 cups water
¼ cup coconut milk
Salt to taste
2 tsp + 3 tsp butter
2 tsp olive oil
2 red peppers, chopped
½ cup baby spinach, chopped

3 mushrooms, chopped
¼ cup broccoli florets, chopped
1/6 cup sliced green onion
½ red onion, chopped
2 cloves garlic, minced
1 medium carrot, grated
⅓ cup almond flour
1 cup unsweetened almond milk
2 tbsp arrowroot starch

Directions

Boil the turnips in a pot over medium heat until tender and mashable. Drain and pour into a bowl. Add 2 teaspoons of butter, coconut milk, and salt. Mash well and set aside.

Place a skillet over medium heat on a stove top and add the remaining vegan butter. Once it melts, add the onion, garlic, red peppers, broccoli, and mushrooms. Stir and cook the veggies for 2 minutes.

Add the green onion and spinach. Cook until the spinach wilts. Season with a bit of salt and stir.

Turn the heat off and pour the veggie mixture in the turnip mash. Use the potato masher to mash the veggies into the turnip. Allow cooling. Using your hands, form balls of the mixture and place them on a baking sheet in a single layer. Refrigerate for 30 minutes.

In 3 separate bowls, pour the pork rinds in one, almond flour in the second bowl, and arrowroot starch, almond milk and salt in the third bowl.

Mix the arrowroot starch with the almond milk and salt with a fork. Remove the patties from the fridge. Preheat the Air Fryer to 390°F.

Dredge each veggie mold in almond flour, then in the arrowroot starch mixture, and then in the pork rinds. Place the patties in batches in a single layer in the fryer basket without overlapping.

Spray them with olive oil cooking spray and cook them for 2 minutes. Flip and spray with cooking spray and continue cooking for 3 minutes. Remove to a wire rack and serve with tomato sauce.

Bacon & Chicken Wrapped Jalapenos

Total Time: 35 min | **Serves**: 6 | **Per serving**: Cal 523; Net Carbs 8.7g; Fat 42.8g; Protein 49.6g

Ingredients

8 jalapeno peppers, halved and seeded
4 chicken breasts, butterflied and halved
6 oz cream cheese
6 oz cheddar cheese

16 slices bacon
1 cup pork rinds, crushed
Salt and black pepper to taste
2 eggs

Directions

Wrap the chicken in cling film and place on a chopping board. Using a rolling pin, pound the chicken evenly to flatten them but not too thin.

Afterward, remove the cling film and season the chicken with pepper and salt on both sides.

In a bowl, add the cream cheese, cheddar cheese, a pinch each of pepper, and salt. Mix well. Take each jalapeno and spoon in the cheese mixture to the brim.

Now, on a chopping board, flatten each piece of chicken and lay 2 bacon slices each on them.

Place a stuffed jalapeno on each laid out chicken and bacon set and wrap the peppers in them. Set aside.

Preheat the Air Fryer to 350°F. Add the eggs to a bowl and pour the pork rinds in another bowl. Also, set a flat plate aside.

Take each wrapped jalapeno and dip it into the eggs and then thoroughly in the pork rinds. Place them on the flat plate.

Open the Air Fryer and lightly grease the fryer basket with cooking spray.

Arrange 4 to 5 jalapenos in the fryer basket, close the Air Fryer and cook for 7 minutes. Prepare a paper towel lined plate and set aside.

Once the timer beeps, open the Air Fryer, turn the jalapenos, close and cook further for 4 minutes.

Once ready, remove them onto the paper towel lined plate and repeat the cooking process for the remaining peppers. Serve with sweet dip.

Paprika Cheesy Sausage Balls

Total Time: 60 min | **Serves**: 6 | **Per serving**: Cal 326; Net Carbs 1g; Fat 26.6g; Protein 19.6g

Ingredients

1 ½ lb ground sausages
2 ¼ cups cheddar cheese, shredded
¾ cups almond flour
½ cup coconut flour
¾ tsp baking soda
4 eggs

¾ cup sour cream
1 tsp dried oregano
1 tsp smoked paprika
2 tsp garlic powder
½ cup melted coconut oil

Directions

Place a pan over medium heat on a stove top, add the sausages and brown for 3-4 minutes. Drain the excess fat derived from cooking and set aside.

Add the baking soda, almond flour, and coconut flour to a bowl. Set aside.

In another bowl, add the eggs, sour cream, oregano, paprika, coconut oil, and garlic powder. Whisk to combine well.

Combine the egg and flour mixtures using a spatula. Add the cheese and sausages. Fold in and let it sit for 5 minutes to thicken.

Rub your hands with coconut oil and mold out bite-size balls out of the batter. Place them on a tray, and refrigerate for 15 minutes.

Remove the sausage balls from the fridge, slide out the fryer basket, and add as much of the balls to it without overcrowding.

Slide the fryer basket in and cook them for 10 minutes per round. Transfer to a serving platter once ready and repeat the cooking process for any remaining balls. Serve with salsa.

Crunchy Kale Chips

Total Time: 10 min | **Serves:** 2 | **Per serving:** Cal 167; Net Carbs 2.9g; Fat 15g; Protein 5g

Ingredients

2 tbsp olive oil
4 cups kale, stemmed
1 tsp vegan seasoning

1 tbsp yeast flakes
Sea salt to taste

Directions

In a bowl, mix the oil, the kale and the vegan seasoning.

Add the yeast and mix well. Dump the coated kale in the Air Fryer's basket.

Set the heat to 370°F and time to 5 minutes. Shake after 3 minutes.

Serve sprinkled with sea salt.

Parmesan Crusted Pickles

Total Time: 35 min | **Serves**: 4 | **Per serving**: Cal 255; Net Carbs 4.2g; Fat 15.5g; Protein 24.7g

Ingredients

3 cups large dill pickles, sliced

2 eggs

2 tsp water

1 cup Parmesan cheese, grated

1 ½ cups pork rinds, crushed

Black pepper to taste

Directions

Add the pork rinds and black pepper to a bowl and mix well. Set aside.

In another bowl, crack the eggs and beat with the water. Set aside.

Add the cheese to a separate bowl. Set aside.

Line a flat surface with a paper towel and arrange the pickle slices on it to extra as much water from them. Preheat the Air Fryer to 400°F.

Pull out the fryer basket and spray it lightly with cooking spray. Dredge the pickle slices it in the egg mixture, then in pork rinds and then in cheese.

Pull out the fryer basket and lay as much coated pickle slices in it without overlapping

Slide the fryer basket back in and cook for 4 minutes.

Open the Air Fryer and turn the pickles over. Cook further for 4 to 5 minutes to make them crispy.

Once ready, remove onto a serving platter and serve with a cheese dip.

Caper Eggplant with Crispy Mozzarella Crust

Total Time: 30 min | **Serves**: 3 | **Per serving**: Cal 317; Net Carbs 2g; Fat 16.8g; Protein 12g

Ingredients

1 cup eggplant, cubed
¼ cup red pepper, chopped
¼ cup green pepper, chopped
¼ cup yellow onion, chopped
⅓ cup tomatoes, chopped
1 clove garlic, minced
1 tbsp pimiento-stuffed olives, sliced

1 tsp capers
¼ tsp dried basil
¼ tsp dried marjoram
Salt and black pepper to taste
¼ cup mozzarella cheese, grated
1 tbsp pork rinds, crushed

Directions

Preheat the Air Fryer to 300°F. In a bowl, add the eggplant, green pepper, red pepper, onion, tomatoes, olives, garlic, basil marjoram, capers, salt, and pepper.

Lightly grease a 3 X 3 inches baking dish with the cooking spray. Ladle the eggplant mixture into the baking dish and level it using the vessel.

Sprinkle the mozzarella cheese on top of it and top it with the pork rinds. Place the dish in the Air Fryer and cook it for 20 minutes.

Avocados Wrapped in Bacon

Total Time: 40 min | **Serves**: 6 | **Per serving**: Cal 193; Net Carbs 2.3g; Fat 18g; Protein 3.4g

Ingredients

12 thick strips bacon
3 large and firm avocados
⅓ tsp salt

⅓ tsp chili powder
⅓ tsp cumin powder

Directions

Using a knife, cut open the avocados, remove the seeds and slice them into 24 pieces without the skin. Set aside.

Stretch the bacon strips to elongate them and use a knife to cut in half to make 24 pieces.

Wrap each piece of bacon around each slice of avocado from one end to the other end. Tuck the end of bacon into the wrap.

Arrange the wrapped avocado on a flat surface and sprinkle with salt, chili and cumin powder on both sides. Slide out the fryer basket and arrange 4 to 8 wrapped pieces in it.

Slide the fryer basket in and cook at 350°F for 8 minutes or until the bacon is browned and crunchy, flipping halfway through to cook evenly.

Remove onto a wire rack and repeat the process for the remaining avocado pieces.

Savory Coconut Shrimp

Total Time: 40 min | **Serves**: 5 | **Per serving**: Cal 260; Net Carbs 2g; Fat 14g; Protein 8g

Ingredients

1 lb jumbo shrimp, peeled and deveined
¾ cup unsweetened coconut, shredded
1 tbsp erythritol
½ cup pork rinds, crushed
⅓ cup arrowroot starch
½ cup coconut milk

Directions

Pour the arrowroot starch in a zipper bag, add the shrimp, zip the pocket up and shake vigorously to coat the shrimp with the arrowroot starch.

Preheat the Air Fryer to 350°F.

Mix the erythritol and coconut milk in a bowl and place it aside.

In a separate bowl, mix the pork rinds and shredded coconut.

Open the zipper bag and remove each shrimp while shaking off excess starch on it.

Dip each shrimp in the coconut milk mixture and then in the pork rinds mixture while pressing loosely to trap enough pork rinds and shredded coconut.

Slide out the fryer basket and place the coated shrimp in it without overcrowding.

Close the Air Fryer and cook the shrimp for 6 to 8 minutes.

Open the Air Fryer, flip the shrimp, and continue cooking for 3 to 4 minutes or until golden brown.

Serve the shrimp with a coconut based dip.

Garlic Calamari Rings

Total Time: 18 min | **Serves**: 2 | **Per serving**: Cal 233; Net Carbs 6.1g; Fat 16.5; Protein 15.2g

Ingredients

½ pound, sliced into rings
¾ cup Parmesan cheese, shredded
2 medium eggs, beaten
1 tsp garlic powder

A pinch of salt
1 cup almond flour
1 tsp paprika powder

Directions

Preheat the Air Fryer to 350°F. Add the eggs to a bowl. Set aside

In another bowl, add the cheese, garlic powder, salt, almond flour, and paprika powder. Mix them using a spoon. Dip each calamari ring in egg, then in the cheese mixture, in the egg again and finally in the cheese mixture.

Slide out the fryer basket and add the rings to it. Cook them for 8 minutes. Remove them onto a serving platter and serve with a cheese or tomatoes dip of choice.

Effortless Mozzarella Sticks

Total Time: 2 hrs 20 min | **Serves**: 4 | **Per serving**: Cal 288; Net Carbs 2.9g; Fat 11g; Protein 39g

Ingredients

12 mozzarella string cheese
2 cups ground pork rinds

3 eggs
4 tbsp coconut milk

Directions

Pour the pork rinds in a medium bowl. Crack the eggs into another bowl and beat with the coconut milk.

One after the other, dip each cheese sticks in the egg mixture, in the pork rinds, then egg mixture again and then in the pork rinds again. Place the coated cheese sticks on a cookie sheet and freeze for 1 to 2 hours.

Preheat the Air Fryer to 380°F.

Pull out the fryer basket and arrange the cheese sticks in it without overcrowding. Slide the fryer basket back in and cook for 5 minutes, flipping them halfway to brown evenly. Remove them to a plate and repeat the cooking process for the remaining sticks.

Italian Salmon Croquettes

Total Time: 40 min | **Serves**: 6 | **Per serving**: Cal 433; Net Carbs 4.1g; Fat 25g; Protein 48.2g

Ingredients

15 oz tinned salmon, deboned and flaked
1 cup grated onion
1 ½ cups grated carrots
3 large eggs
1 ½ tbsp chives, chopped

4 tbsp mayonnaise
4 tbsp pork rinds, crushed
2 ½ tsp Italian seasoning
Salt and black pepper to taste
2 ½ tsp lemon juice

Directions

In a mixing bowl, add the salmon, onion, carrots, eggs, chives, mayonnaise, pork rinds, Italian seasoning, pepper, salt, and lemon juice and mix well.

Using your hands, form 2-inch thick oblong balls from the mixture of as much as you can get. Put the croquettes on a flat tray and refrigerate for 45 minutes to make compact. Pull out the fryer basket and grease with cooking spray.

Remove the croquettes from the fridge and arrange in the fryer basket without overcrowding. Re-spray with cooking spray. Slide the fryer basket in and cook for 6 minutes at 390°F until crispy.

Flip the patties, spray with oil, and continue cooking for 4 minutes. Once ready, transfer the croquettes to a serving platter and serve with a dill dip.

Pin Wheel

Total Time: 6 min | **Serves**: 4 | **Per serving:** Cal 392; Net Carbs 3.2g; Fat 35g; Protein 15g

Ingredients

2 lb dill pickles
1 lb cream cheese, softened
3 oz ham, sliced

2 almond tortillas
Salt and black pepper, to taste

Directions

Spread the cream cheese on one side of the tortilla. Put a slice of ham over it. Spread a layer of cheese on top of the ham. Roll 1 pickle up in the tortilla.

Preheat the Air Fryer to 340°F. Place the rolls in the basket of the Air Fryer and cook for 6 minutes.

Spicy Chicken Wings

Total Time: 45 min | **Serves**: 3 | **Per serving**: Cal 295; Net Carbs 1.8g; Fat 21g; Protein 35g

Ingredients

15 chicken wings
Salt and black pepper to taste
⅓ cup hot sauce

⅓ cup butter
½ tbsp white vinegar

Directions

Preheat the Air Fryer to 360°F. Season the wings with pepper and salt.

Slide out the fryer basket, add the wings to it and cook for 35 minutes. Toss them every 5 minutes.

Once read, remove them into a bowl. Over low heat on a stove top, place a saucepan, add the butter and melt it. Add the vinegar and hot sauce. Stir and cook for a minute. Turn the heat off.

Pour the sauce over the chicken. Toss to coat well. Transfer the chicken to a serving platter. Serve with a side of celery strips and blue cheese dressing.

Chili Calamari with Olives

Total Time: 25 min | **Serves**: 3 | **Per serving**: Cal 218; Net Carbs 5.3g; Fat 16.5g; Protein 4.6g

Ingredients

½ lb calamari rings
½ piece coriander, chopped
2 strips chili pepper, chopped

1 tbsp olive oil
1 cup pimiento stuffed green olives, sliced
Salt and black pepper to taste

Directions

In a bowl, add the calamari rings, chili pepper, salt, black pepper, oil, and coriander.

Mix and leave the calamari to marinate for 10 minutes. Pour the calamari into an oven-safe bowl, good enough to fit into the fryer basket. Slide the fryer basket out, place the bowl in it, and slide the basket back in. Cook the calamari for 15 minutes at 390°F, stirring every 5 minutes using a spoon.

After 15 minutes, open the Air Fryer, and add the olives. Stir, close the Air Fryer and continue cooking for 3 minutes. Once ready, transfer to a serving platter. Serve warm.

Delicious Mixed Nuts

Total Time: 25 min | **Serves**: 6 | **Per serving**: Cal 170; Net Carbs 3g; Fat 15g; Protein 6g

Ingredients

½ cup pecans
½ cup walnuts
½ cup almonds
A pinch ground cayenne pepper

2 tbsp stevia sweetener
2 tbsp egg whites
2 tsp cinnamon powder

Directions

Preheat Air Fryer to 300°F.

Add the pepper, stevia, and cinnamon to a bowl and mix them well. Set aside.

In another bowl, pour in the pecans, walnuts, almonds, and egg whites. Mix well. Add the spice mixture to the nuts and give it a good mix.

Open the Air Fryer and lightly grease the fryer basket with cooking spray. Pour in the nuts, close the Air Fryer, and bake them for 10 minutes. Open the Air Fryer, stir the nuts using a wooden vessel, close the Air Fryer, and bake further for 10 minutes.

Set a bowl ready and once the timer is done, pour the nuts in the bowl. Let cool before crunching on them as they are.

Carrot Crisps

Total Time: 20 min | **Serves**: 2 | **Per serving**: Cal 35; Net Carbs 6g; Fat 0g; Protein 1g

Ingredients

3 large carrots, washed and peeled

Salt to taste

Directions

Using a mandolin slicer, slice the carrots very thinly heightwise.

Put the carrot strips in a bowl and season with salt to taste.

Open the Air Fryer, grease the fryer basket lightly with cooking spray, and add the carrot strips to it. Close the Air Fryer and fry at 350°F for 6 minutes.

Pull out the fryer basket, and stir the carrots with a spoon. Cook further for 4 minutes or until crispy. Serve with dipping sauce of your choice.

Ginger Beef Meatballs

Total Time: 25 min | **Serves**: 3 | **Per serving**: Cal 221; Net Carbs 2.4g; Fat 13g; Protein 23g

Ingredients

½ lb ground beef
1 small finger ginger, crushed
1 tbsp hot sauce
3 tbsp vinegar
1 ½ tsp lemon juice

½ cup tomato ketchup, reduced sugar
2 tbsp erythritol
¼ tsp dry mustard
Salt and black pepper to taste

Directions

In a bowl, add the beef, ginger, hot sauce, vinegar, lemon juice, tomato ketchup, erythritol, dry mustard, pepper, and salt and mix well using a spoon.

Mold out 2-inch sized balls out of the mixture with your hands. Pull out the fryer basket and add the balls to it without overcrowding. Slide the fryer basket back in and cook the balls at 370°F for 15 minutes. Remove them onto a serving platter and repeat the frying process for any remaining balls.

Serve with a tomato or cheese dip.

Cilantro Cheese Balls

Total Time: 50 min | **Serves**: 6 | **Per serving**: Cal 176; Net Carbs 5g; Fat 15g; Protein 5g

Ingredients

2 cups crumbled cottage cheese
2 cups Parmesan cheese, grated
2 turnips, peeled and chopped
1 medium onion, finely chopped
1 ½ tsp red chili flakes

1 green chili, finely chopped
Salt to taste
4 tbsp cilantro leaves, chopped
1 cup almond flour
1 cup pork rinds, crushed

Directions

Place the turnips in a pot, add water and bring them to boil over medium heat on a stove top for 25 to 30 minutes until soft.

Turn off the heat, drain the turnips through a sieve, and place in a bowl. With a potato masher, mash the turnips and leave to cool.

Now, add the cottage cheese, parmesan cheese, onion, red chili flakes, green chili, salt, coriander, and almond flour to the turnip mash.

Mix the ingredients well, then, mold out bite-size balls. Pour the pork rinds in a bowl and roll each cheese ball lightly in it. Place them on a tray.

Preheat Air Fryer to 350°F. Open it and place 8 to 10 cheese balls in the fryer basket.

Close the fryer and cook them for 15 minutes.

Once ready, remove to a plate.

Repeat the cooking process for the remaining balls. Serve with tomato-based dip.

Tortilla Chips

Total Time: 55 min | **Serves**: 3 | **Per serving**: Cal 165; Net Carbs 3g; Fat 14.4g; Protein 4.7g

Ingredients

1 cup almond flour
Salt and black pepper to taste

1 tbsp golden flaxseed meal
2 cups cheddar cheese, shredded

Directions

Preheat the Air Fryer to 350°F.

Pour the cheddar cheese in a medium sized microwave safe dish and melt it in the microwave for 1 minute. Remove the bowl in 15-second intervals to stir the cheese.

Once melted, remove the bowl and quickly add the almond flour, salt, flaxseed meal, and pepper. Mix well with a fork.

On a chopping board, place the dough, and knead it with your hands while warm until the ingredients are well combined.

Divide the dough into two and using a rolling pin, roll them out flat into two rectangles.

Use a pastry cutter, to cut out triangle-shaped pieces and line them in 1 layer on a baking dish.

Open the Air Fryer and grease the fryer basket lightly with cooking spray.

Arrange some triangle chips in 1 layer in the fryer basket without touching or overlapping. Spray with cooking spray.

Close the Air Fryer and cook for 8 minutes.

Smoked Paprika Zucchini Parmesan Chips

Total Time: 70 min | **Serves**: 4 | **Per serving**: Cal 140; Net Carbs 1g; Fat 9g; Protein 4g

Ingredients

3 medium zucchinis
1 cup pork rinds, crushed
2 eggs, beaten

1 cup grated Parmesan cheese
Salt and black pepper to taste
1 tsp smoked paprika

Directions

With a mandolin cutter, slice the zucchinis thinly. Use paper towels to press out excess liquid.

In a bowl, add the pork rinds, salt, pepper, cheese, and paprika. Mix well and set aside. Place a wire rack or tray. Set aside.

Now, dip each zucchini slice in egg and then in the cheese mix while pressing to coat them well in cheese. Place them on the wire rack.

Spray the coated slices with cooking spray. Open the Air Fryer, place the slices in the fryer basket in a single layer without overlapping.

Close the Air Fryer and cook them at 350°F for 8 minutes for each batch. Once ready, remove them onto a serving platter and sprinkle with salt.

Bread Cheese Sticks

Total Time: 5 min | **Serves**: 3 | **Per serving**: Cal 112; Net Carbs 1g; Fat 10g; Protein 6g

Ingredients

6 (6 oz) bread cheese

2 tbsp butter

Directions

Put the butter in a bowl and melt it in the microwave, for about 2 minutes. Set aside.

Cut the cheese into equal sized sticks. Brush each stick with butter. Arrange the coated cheese sticks in a single layer on the fryer basket.

Slide in the fryer basket and cook at 390°F for 10 minutes. Flip halfway to brown evenly.

Serve with a tomato dip.

Air Fried Radish Chips

Total Time: 35 min | **Serves**: 4 | **Per serving**: Cal 48; Net Carbs 0.2g; Fat 2.7g; Protein 0.8g

Ingredients

10 Radishes, leaves removed, cleaned   Salt to taste

Directions

With a mandolin slicer, slice the radishes thinly.

Place the radishes in a pot and pour in water to cover them up. Place the pot over medium heat and bring the water to boil until the radishes turn translucent about 4 minutes.

Drain the radishes through a sieve. Set aside. Open the Air Fryer and grease the fryer basket with cooking spray. Add the radish slices into the fryer basket. Close the air fryer, and cook for 8 minutes at 390°F or until they are a deep golden brown color.

Meanwhile, prepare a paper towel-lined plate. Once the radishes are ready, transfer them to the paper towel-lined plate. Season with salt and serve.

Almond Onion Rings

Total Time: 10 min | **Serves**: 3 | **Per serving:** Cal 165; Net Carbs 4.7g; Fat 8g; Protein 6g

Ingredients

1 onion   1 egg
1 ½ cups almond flour   1 cup coconut milk
1 tbsp baking powder   ¾ cup pork rinds, crushed , crushed

Directions

Preheat the Air Fryer for 10 minutes, if needed.

Cut the onion into slices and then separate them into rings. In a bowl, add the flour, the baking powder, and the salt.

Whisk the eggs and the milk and combine with the flour. Dip the floured onion rings into the batter to coat it.

Spread the pork rinds on a plate and dredge all the rings in the rinds. Cook the rings in the Air Fryer for around 10 minutes at 360°F.

Chili Cheese Lings

Total Time: 25 min | **Serves**: 4 | **Per serving**: Cal 112; Net Carbs 3.1g; Fat 5.6g; Protein 2.8g

Ingredients

4 tbsp grated cheddar cheese + extra for rolling

1 cup almond flour + extra for kneading

¼ tsp chili powder

½ tsp baking powder

3 tsp butter

A pinch of salt

Directions

In a bowl, add the cheese, almond flour, baking powder, chili powder, butter, and salt. Mix well. The mixture should be crusty.

Add some drops of water and mix well to get a dough. Remove the dough to a chopping board. Rub some extra flour in your palms and knead the dough for a while.

Sprinkle some more flour on the flat surface and using a rolling pin, roll the dough out into a thin sheet. With a pastry cutter, cut the dough into your desired shapes.

Preheat the Air Fryer to 350°F.

Pull out the fryer basket and add the cheese lings. Close the Air Fryer and cook for 2 minutes. Open the Air Fryer, toss the cheese lings, and continue cooking for 3 minutes.

Mouth-Watering Salami Sticks

Total Time: 140 min | **Serves**: 2 | **Per serving**: Cal 418; Net Carbs 0.5g; Fat 32.5g; Protein 29.2g

Ingredients

1 lb ground beef or pork

3 tbsp erythritol

A pinch garlic powder

A pinch chili powder

Salt to taste

1 tsp liquid smoke

Directions

Place the meat, erythritol, garlic powder, chili powder, salt and liquid smoke in a bowl. Mix with a spoon. Mold out four sticks with your hands, place them on a plate, and refrigerate approximately for 2 hours.

Preheat the Air Fryer to 350°F. Slide out the fryer basket and add the salami sticks to it. Cook for 10 minutes. Serve with a dipping sauce of choice

Portobello Mushroom Melts

Total Time: 25 min | **Serves**: 2 | **Per serving:** Cal 243; Net Carbs 2g; Fat 16g; Protein 13g

Ingredients

1 tbsp olive oil

1 tsp balsamic vinegar

1 oz mushrooms, sliced

¼ large red onion, sliced

Salt and black pepper

3 flaxseed tortillas

2 oz cream cheese

2 tbsp pesto sauce

½ tomato

2 oz mozzarella cheese

Directions

Preheat the Air Fryer to 390°F.

Mix olive oil and balsamic vinegar. Add the mushrooms and the onion. Season with salt and black pepper. Cook for 5 minutes. Remove from the Fryer, then lower the temperature to 330°F. Brush each side of the tortillas with olive oil.

Top the tortillas with cream cheese, mushrooms and onions. Spread the pesto on the tortillas and press against the mushrooms. Top with tomato, cheese and cook for 7 minutes.

Celery Salmon Balls

Total Time: 15 min | **Serves**: 2 | **Per serving:** Cal 389; Net Carbs 1.6g; Fat 32g; Protein 25g

Ingredients

6 oz tinned salmon

1 large egg

4 tbsp celery, chopped

4 tbsp spring onion, sliced

1 tbsp fresh dill, chopped

½ tbsp garlic powder

5 tbsp pork rinds, crushed

3 tbsp olive oil

Directions

Preheat the Air Fryer to 370°F.

In a large bowl, mix salmon, egg, celery, onion, dill, and garlic powder. Shape the mixture into golf ball size balls and roll them in pork rinds.

Heat the oil in a skillet. Add the salmon balls and slowly flatten them. Then transfer them to the Air Fryer and fry for about 10 minutes.

Mozzarella & Pepperoni Mushrooms

Total Time: 9 min | **Serves:** 3 | **Per serving:** Cal 340; Net Carbs 3.8g; Fat 19g; Protein 37g

Ingredients

3 portobello mushrooms, stems removed
3 tbsp olive oil
3 tbsp tomato sauce
3 tbsp mozzarella cheese, shredded
12 slices pepperoni

A pinch of salt
A pinch of dried Italian seasonings
Flakes red pepper, crushed for garnish
Parmesan cheese, for garnish

Directions

Preheat the Air Fryer to 330°F. Drizzle a little bit of olive oil on each side of the mushroom.

Season the inside of each mushroom with salt and Italian seasonings. Spread tomato sauce evenly over the mushrooms and top with cheese.

Place the stuffed mushrooms in the cooking basket and insert in the Air Fryer.

After just 1 minute, remove the basket from the Air Fryer and add the pepperoni slices on top of the portobello pizza. Place back on the fire and cook for 5 more minutes.

Finish the dish by topping with grated Parmesan cheese and red pepper flakes.

Cauliflower & Mushroom Balls

Total Time: 50 min | **Serves**: 6 | **Per serving**: Cal 95; Net Carbs 3g; Fat 5.8g; Protein 5.6g

Ingredients

½ lb mushrooms, diced
3 tbsp olive oil
1 small red onion, chopped
3 cloves garlic, minced
3 cups cauli rice
2 tbsp vegetable stock

1 cup pork rinds, crushed
1 cup Grana Padano cheese
¼ cup coconut oil
2 sprigs fresh thyme, chopped
Salt and black pepper to taste

Directions

Place a skillet over medium heat on a stove top. Add olive oil, once heated add the garlic and onion. Sauté until translucent.

Add the mushrooms, stir and cook for about 4 minutes.

Add the cauli rice and constantly stir-fry for 5 minutes. Add the chicken stock, thyme, and simmer until the cauli rice has absorbed the stock.

Add Grana Padano cheese, pepper, and salt. Stir and turn off the heat.

Allow the mixture cool and make bite-size balls of the mix. Place them in a plate and refrigerate them for 30 minutes to harden.

Preheat the Air Fryer to 350°F.

In a bowl, add the pork rinds and coconut oil and mix well. Remove the mushroom balls from the refrigerator, stir the pork rind mixture again, and roll the balls in the pork rind mixture.

Place the balls in the fryer basket without overcrowding and cook for 15 minutes while tossing every 5 minutes for an even cook.

Repeat this process until all the mushroom balls have fried.

Beef Liver with Eggs

Total Time: 15 min | **Serves**: 4 | **Per serving:** Cal 287; Net Carbs 1.2g; Fat 23g; Protein 12g

Ingredients

2 large eggs
½ lb beef liver, sliced
Salt and black pepper, to taste
1 tbsp butter
½ tbsp black truffle oil
1 tbsp cream cheese

Directions

Preheat the Air Fryer to 340°F.

Cut the liver into thin slices and put in the fridge. Separate whites the yolks, and put each yolk in a cup.

In another bowl, add the cream cheese, the truffle oil, salt, and black pepper and beat the combined mixture with a fork.

Take the liver and arrange ½ of the mixture in a small ramekin. Pour the white of the egg and divide it equally between ramekins. Put the yolks on top.

Surround each yolk with the liver and cook for 12 minutes. Serve cold.

Garlic Roasted Vegetables with Olives

Total Time: 12 min | **Serves:** 4 | **Per serving:** Cal 212; Net Carbs 7.8g; Fat 13g; Protein 10g

Ingredients

1 lb tomatoes
1 lb green pepper
1 medium onion, chopped
3 cloves garlic
½ tbsp salt

1 tbsp coriander powder
1 tbsp lemon juice
1 tbsp olive oil
2 oz black olive
3 cooked eggs

Directions

Line the pepper, tomatoes and onion in the basket. Cook for 5 minutes, then flip around and cook for 5 more minutes, at 300°F. Remove them from the Air Fryer and peel their skin.

Place the vegetables in a blender and sprinkle with the salt and the coriander powder. Blend to a smooth mixture. Top with the cooked eggs and sprinkle olive oil.

Hot Almond Flour Cheesy Lings

Total Time: 5 min | **Serves:** 4 | **Per serving:** Cal 173; Net Carbs 2.5g; Fat 14g; Protein 6g

Ingredients

1 cup almond flour
1 tsp baking powder
¼ tsp chili powder

1 tsp butter
3 tbsp cheddar cheese, grated
Hot sauce, to serve

Directions

Mix the flour and the baking powder. Add salt, chili powder, butter, grated cheese, and a few drops of water to the mixture. Make sure to make a stiff dough.

Knead the dough for a while.

Now, sprinkle a small quantity of flour on the table. Take a rolling pin and roll the dough. Then, cut into any shape wanted.

Preheat the Air Fryer to 370°F. Set the time to 4 minutes and line the cheese lings in the basket. Serve with hot sauce.

Cheddar Cheese Croquettes with Prosciutto

Total Time: 45 min | **Serves:** 6 | **Per serving:** Cal 346; Net Carbs 5.2g; Fat 25g; Protein 23g

Ingredients

1 lb. cheddar cheese, sliced
12 slices prosciutto
1 cup almond flour

2 eggs, beaten
4 tbsp olive oil
1 cup pork rinds, crushed

Directions

Wrap each slice of cheese with 2 prosciutto slices. Place them in the freezer just enough to set. Preheat your Air Fryer to 380°F.

Dip the croquettes into the flour first then the egg, and then coat them with the pork rinds.

Place the olive oil in the basket of the Air Fryer and cook the croquettes for 7 minutes, or until golden.

Speedy Cheesy Strips

Total Time: 40-45 min | **Serves:** 3 | **Per serving:** Cal 314; Net Carbs 1.5g; Fat 16g; Protein 36g

Ingredients

8 oz mozzarella cheese
1 tsp garlic powder
1 egg
1 cup pork rinds, crushed
½ tsp salt
2 tbsp olive oil

Directions

Cut the mozzarella into 6 strips. Whisk the egg along with the salt and garlic powder.

Dip the mozzarella into the egg mixture first, and then into the pork rinds.

Arrange them on a platter and place in the freezer for about 30 min.

Preheat the Air Fryer to 360°F. Drizzle olive oil into the Air Fryer.

Arrange the mozzarella sticks in the Air Fryer and cook for 5 minutes. Flip at least twice, to ensure that they will cook evenly on all sides.

The Best Chili Rellenos

Total Time: 35 min | **Serves:** 5 | **Per serving:** Cal 258; Net Carbs 2g; Fat 20g; Protein 15g

Ingredients

2 cans green chili peppers
1 cup Monterey Jack Cheese
1 cup cheddar cheese, shredded
2 large eggs, beaten

½ cup water
2 tbsp almond flour
½ cup milk
1 can tomato sauce

Directions

Preheat the Air Fryer to 350°F. Spray a baking dish with the cooking spray.

Take half of the chilies and arrange them in the baking dish. Top chilies with cheddar cheese and cover with the remaining chilies.

In a bowl, combine the eggs, the water, the flour. Pour the mixture over the chilies. Fry for 25 minutes. Remove the chilies from the Air Fryer, and pour the tomato sauce over.

Cook again for 10 minutes. Top with the Monterey jack cheese, to serve.

Parmesan Asparagus Fries

Total Time: 32 min | **Serves:** 4 | **Per serving:** Cal 213; Net Carbs 4.1g; Fat 12g; Protein 19g

Ingredients

1 lb. asparagus spears
¼ cup almond flour
1 cup pork rinds, crushed

½ cup Parmesan cheese, grated
2 eggs, beaten
Salt and black pepper, to taste

Directions

Preheat the Air Fryer to 380°F.

Combine the pork rinds and the Parmesan cheese in a small bowl. Season with salt and pepper.

Line a baking sheet with parchment paper.

Dip half of the asparagus spears into the flour, then into the eggs, and finally coat with pork rinds. Arrange them on the sheet and cook for about 9 to 10 minutes.

Repeat with the remaining spears.

Sunday Cooked Tomato Nest

Total Time: 20 min | **Serves:** 2 | **Per serving:** Cal 302; Net Carbs 4.2g; Fat 16g; Protein 30g

Ingredients

2 tomatoes
4 eggs
1 cup mozzarella cheese, shredded

a few basil leaves
1 tbsp olive oil
Salt and black pepper, to taste

Directions

Preheat the Air Fryer to 360°F.

Cut each tomato into two halves and place them in a bowl. Season with salt and pepper. Place cheese around the bottom of the tomatoes and add basil leaves.

Break one egg in each tomato slice. Top with cheese and drizzle with olive oil. Set the temperature to 360°F and cook for 20 minutes.

Salmon with Dill Sauce

Total Time: 28 min | **Serves:** 2 | **Per serving:** Cal 291; Net Carbs 5.6g; Fat 23g; Protein 15g

Ingredients

2 pieces salmon, 6 oz each
2 tbsp olive oil

A pinch of salt

Dill sauce:

½ cup full-fat Greek yogurt
½ cup sour cream

A pinch of salt
2 tbsp fresh dill, finely chopped

Directions

Preheat the Air Fryer to 270°F.

Cut the salmon into four equal sized portions then drizzle with oil. Season with a pinch of sea salt.

Place the seasoned salmon into the Air Fryer's cooking basket. Cook for 20-25 minutes and top with dill sauce.

For the dill sauce: in a large mixing bowl, combine the yogurt, the sour cream, the chopped dill, and salt. Beat well until smooth.

Homemade Broccoli with Cheese

Total Time: 20 min | **Serves:** 3 | **Per serving:** Cal 432; Net Carbs 3.2g; Fat 37g; Protein 24g

Ingredients

1 head broccoli
4 eggs
1 cup cream cheese
A pinch of nutmeg

1 tbsp ginger powder
1 cup cheddar cheese, shredded
Salt and black pepper to taste

Directions

Cook the broccoli on steam for around 4 minutes. Drain the broccoli and combine with one egg and the cream cheese. Add the nutmeg, the ginger, salt, and pepper.

Butter several small ramekins and spread the mixture. Sprinkle cheese on top. Set the timer to 20 minutes and cook at 220°F.

Crispy Eggplant Fries

Total Time: 20 min | **Serves:** 3 | **Per serving:** Cal 265; Net Carbs 4,2g; Fat 21g; Protein 4g

Ingredients

2 eggplants
¼ cup almond flour

¼ cup olive oil
½ cup water

Directions

Preheat the Air Fryer to 390°F. Cut the eggplants in slices of half inch each.

In a big bowl, mix the flour, olive oil, water, and the eggplants. Slowly coat the eggplants. Cook for around 12 minutes or until they start to brown. Repeat this process until all eggplant slices are cooked. Serve with yogurt or tomato sauce.

Crispy Crumbed Chicken Tenderloins

Total Time: 15 min | **Serves:** 4 | **Per serving:** Cal 312; Net Carbs 0.8g; Fat 17g; Protein 21g

Ingredients

2 tbsp oil
2 oz pork rinds, crushed

1 large egg, whisked
6 chicken tenderloins

Directions

Preheat the Air Fryer to 365°F. Combine the oil with the pork rinds. Keep mixing and stirring until the mixture gets crumbly.

Dip the chicken in the egg wash. Dip the chicken in the rinds mix, making sure it is evenly and fully covered. Cook for 12 minutes. Serve the dish and enjoy its crispy taste!

Garlic Fried Tomatoes

Total Time: 20 min | **Serves**: 2 | **Per serving:** Cal 135; Net Carbs 6.7g; Fat 5g; Protein 1g

Ingredients

4 tomatoes
1 tbsp olive oil
Salt and black pepper, to taste

1 clove garlic, minced
½ tbsp dried thyme
3 tbsp vinegar

Directions

Preheat the Air Fryer to 390°F. Cut the tomatoes in half, and remove the seeds.

Put them in a big bowl and toss well with the oil, the salt, the pepper, the garlic, and the thyme. Place them in the Air Fryer and cook them for 15 minutes. Drizzle with vinegar and serve.

Simple Zucchini Fries

Total Time: 15 min | **Serves**: 3 | **Per serving:** Cal 193; Net Carbs 0.3g; Fat 21g; Protein 1g

Ingredients

4 large zucchini
¼ cup almond flour
¼ cup olive oil

¼ cup water
A pinch of salt

Directions

Preheat the Air Fryer to 390°F. Cut the zucchini to a half inch by 3 inches. In a large bowl, mix the flour, the olive oil, the water, and the zucchini.

Mix very well and coat the zucchini. Line the zucchini fries in the Air Fryer and cook for 15 minutes. Recommended to serving with Greek yogurt and garlic paste.

Famous Fried Calamari

Total Time: 10 min | **Serves:** 4 | **Per serving:** Cal 233; Net Carbs 0.7g; Fat 11g; Protein 32g

Ingredients

1 lb calamari (squid), cut in rings
¼ cup almond flour

2 large eggs, beaten
1 cup pork rinds, crushed

Directions

Coat the calamari rings with the flour. Dip the calamari in the mixture of the eggs. Then, dip in the pork rinds. Cool in the fridge for 2 hours.

Line them in the Air Fryer and apply oil generously. Cook for 10 minutes at 380°F. Serve with garlic mayo or lemon wedges.

Lemon Bacon Shrimp

Total Time: 10 min | **Serves:** 16 | **Per serving:** Cal 125; Net Carbs 1.2g; Fat 10g; Protein 11g

Ingredients

1 ¼ lbs shrimp, peeled, 16 pieces
1 lb bacon, 16 slices

Juice from 1 lemon

Directions

Take a slice of bacon and carefully wrap it around one shrimp, starting from the shrimp's head. Put the wrapped shrimps into the fridge for 25 minutes.

Preheat the Air Fryer to 390°F. Cook them for 6 – 8 minutes. Sprinkle with lemon juice and serve.

Family Calamari Rings

Total Time: 25 min / **Serves:** 3 | **Per serving:** Cal 128; Net Carbs 0g; Fat 3g; Protein 22g

Ingredients

½ lb calamari rings
½ piece coriander, chopped
2 strips chili pepper, chopped

1 tbsp olive oil
1 cup pimiento-stuffed green olives, sliced
Salt and black pepper to taste

Directions

In a bowl, add rings, chili pepper, salt, black pepper, oil, and coriander. Mix and let marinate for 10 minutes. Pour the calamari into an oven-safe bowl, that fits into the fryer basket.

Slide the fryer basket out, place the bowl in it, and slide the basket back in. Cook for 15 minutes stirring every 5 minutes using a spoon, at 400 F. After 15 minutes, and add in the olives.

Stir, close and continue to cook for 3 minutes.

Once ready, transfer to a serving platter. Serve warm with a side of bread slices and mayonnaise.

Veggie Spring Rolls

Total Time: 30 min | **Serves:** 8 | **Per serving:** Cal 88; Net Carbs 7.2g; Fat 3.1g; Protein 2g

Ingredients

8 grape leaves
7 ounces cooked shirataki fettuccini noodles
2 garlic cloves, chopped
1 tbsp fresh ginger, minced
2 tbsp soy sauce, sugar-free

1 tsp sesame oil
1 red bell pepper, seeds removed, chopped
1 cup mushrooms, chopped
1 cup carrot, chopped
½ cup scallions, chopped

Directions

In a saucepan, add garlic, ginger, soy sauce, pepper, mushroom, carrot and scallions, and stir-fry over high heat for a few minutes, until soft.

Add in shirataki fettuccini noodles and remove from the heat.

Place the grape leaves onto a working board. Spoon dollop of veggie and noodle mixture at the center of each grape leaf.

Roll the spring rolls and tuck the corners and edges in to create neat and secure rolls.

Spray with cooking spray and transfer to the air fryer. Cook for 12 minutes at 340°F, turning once halfway through cooking. Cook until golden and crispy.

Serve with chili sauce.

Thyme Meatballs in Tomato Sauce

Total Time: 23 min | **Serves:** 3 | **Per serving:** Cal 441; Net Carbs 3.2g; Fat 37g; Protein 22g

Ingredients

1 medium onion, chopped
12 oz ground beef meat
1 tbsp fresh parsley, chopped
½ tbsp thyme leaves, chopped

1 egg
3 tbsp pork rinds, crushed
Salt and black pepper to taste
6 oz tomato sauce

Directions

Place the ingredients except for the tomato sauce into a bowl and mix very well. Shape the mixture into 10 to 12 balls.

Preheat the Air Fryer to 390°F. Place the meatballs in the Air Fryer basket, and cook for 8-9 minutes.

Remove the meatballs and transfer to an oven plate. Add in the tomato sauce and place in the Air Fryer. Cook again at 330°F for 4 minutes.

Favorite Eggplant Caviar

Total Time: 20 min | **Serves:** 3 | **Per serving:** Cal 287; Net Carbs 5.2g; Fat 7g; Protein 4g

Ingredients

2 medium eggplants
½ red onion

1½ tbsp balsamic vinegar
1 tbsp olive oil

Directions

Preheat the Air Fryer. Wash, then dry the eggplants.

Arrange them in a plate and cook them for 20 minutes at 360°F. Remove the eggplants from the oven and let cool down. Blend the onion in a blender.

Cut the eggplants in half, lengthwise, and empty their insides with a spoon.

Put the inside of the eggplants in the mixer and process everything.

Add vinegar, olive oil and a little bit of salt, then blend again.

Serve cool with tomato sauce or ketchup.

Directions

Cut the tomatoes in half and arranges them in the Air Fryer. Sprinkle with ground black pepper and salt. Add dried herbs of your choice. Top with cheese. Add parsley, basil, oregano, thyme, rosemary, and sage.

Set the timer to 20 minutes and the heat to 320°F. Serve warm and enjoy!

Persian Garlic Mushrooms

Total Time: 20 min | **Serves:** 4 | **Per serving:** Cal 240; Net Carbs 7.2g; Fat 19g; Protein 10g

Ingredients

6 portobello mushrooms
3 oz butter, softened
2 large shallots
2 cloves garlic

1 tbsp fresh parsley, chopped
A pinch of salt
A pinch of pepper
1 cup parmesan cheese, grated

Directions

Preheat the Air Fryer to 390°F.

Clean the mushrooms and remove the stems. Slice the shallots and the garlic.

Place the mushroom stems, the garlic and the shallots, the parsley and the softened butter in a blender. Arrange the caps of the mushrooms in the basket of the Air Fryer. Stuff the caps with the mixture and sprinkle with Parmesan cheese. Set the timer to 20 minutes.

Herby Turnip Chips

Total Time: 60 min | **Serves:** 2 | **Per serving:** Cal 162; Net Carbs 6.2g; Fat 14g; Protein 1.4g

Ingredients

3 turnips, sliced
2 tbsp olive oil
3 garlic cloves, crushed

1 tsp each of fresh rosemary, thyme, oregano, chopped
Salt and black pepper to taste

Directions

In a bowl, add oil, garlic, herbs, salt and pepper and toss with hands until well-coated.

Arrange the slices in the air fryer's basket and cook for 14 minutes at 360°F, shaking it every 4-5 minutes. Enjoy with onion dip.

Sticky Ginger-Garlic Beef Ribs with Hot Sauce

Total Time: 35 min | **Serves**: 2 | **Per serving**: Cal 616; Net Carbs 2.4g; Fat 53g; Protein 41.7g

Ingredients

1 rack rib steak
Kosher salt to season
1 tsp white pepper
1 tsp garlic powder

½ tsp red pepper flakes
1 tsp ginger powder
½ cup hot sauce

Directions

Preheat the Air Fryer to 360°F.

Place the rib rack on a flat surface and pat dry using a paper towel. Season the ribs with salt, garlic, ginger, white pepper, and red pepper flakes. Place in the fryer basket and cook for 15 minutes.

Turn the ribs with kitchen tongs and cook further for 15 minutes. Remove the ribs onto a chopping board and let it sit for 3 minutes before slicing. Plate and drizzle hot sauce over and serve.

Best-Ever Stuffed Mushrooms

Total Time: 30 min | **Serves**: 10 | **Per serving**: Cal 65; Net Carbs 3.2g; Fat 4.5g; Protein 3.4g

Ingredients

10 mushrooms, stems removed
Olive oil to brush the mushrooms
1 cup cauli rice

1 cup Grana Padano cheese, grated
1 tsp dried mixed herbs
Salt and black pepper to taste

Directions

Brush every mushroom with oil and lay onto a board.

In a bowl, mix cauli rice, cheese, herbs, salt and pepper. Stuff the mushrooms with the mixture.

Arrange the mushrooms in the air fryer and cook for 14 minutes at 360°F. Once ready, make sure the mushrooms cooked until golden and the cheese has melted.

Serve with herbs scattered about.

Goat Cheese & Pancetta Bombs with Plums

Total Time: 25 min | **Serves:** 15 | **Per serving:** Cal 151; Net Carbs 8.2g; Fat 10.5g; Protein 9g

Ingredients

16 oz soft goat cheese
2 tbsp fresh rosemary, finely chopped
1 cup almonds, chopped into small pieces

Salt and black pepper to taste
15 dried plums, chopped
15 pancetta slices

Directions

Line the air fryer with baking paper.

In a bowl, add cheese, rosemary, almonds, salt, pepper and plums and stir well.

Roll into balls and wrap with a pancetta slice. Arrange the bombs in the air fryer and cook for 10 minutes at 400°F. Check at the 5-minute mark, to avoid overcooking.

When ready, let cool before removing them from the air fryer.

Serve on a platter with toothpicks!

Creole Fried Tomatoes

Total Time: 15 min | **Serves:** 3 | **Per serving:** Cal 123; Net Carbs 3.1g; Fat 18g; Protein 5.3g

Ingredients

1 green tomato, sliced
¼ tbsp Creole seasoning
Salt and black pepper to taste

¼ cup almond flour
½ cup buttermilk
Pork rinds as needed

Directions

Add almond flour to one bowl and buttermilk another. Season the tomatoes with salt and pepper.

Make a mix of creole seasoning and pork rinds. Cover tomato slices with almond flour, dip in buttermilk and then into the pork rinds. Do the same for all the slices.

Preheat your Air Fryer to 400°F. Place the tomato slices in your air fryer's cooking basket and cook for 5 minutes.

Serve and enjoy!

Easy Meatballs with Herbs

Total Time: 30 min | **Serves:** 3 | **Per serving:** Cal 483; Net Carbs 8.2g; Fat 23g; Protein 54g

Ingredients

1 lb. ground beef
1 onion, finely chopped
3 garlic cloves, finely chopped
2 eggs

1 cup pork rinds, crushed
½ cup fresh mixed herbs
Salt and pepper to taste
Olive oil

Directions

In a bowl, add beef, onion, garlic, eggs, pork rinds, herbs, salt and pepper and mix with hands to combine. Shape into balls and arrange them in the air fryer's basket.

Drizzle with oil and cook for 16 minutes at 380°F, turning once halfway through cooking.

Cayenne Peppered Parsnip Fries

Total Time: 25 min | **Serves:** 4 | **Per serving:** Cal 104; Net Carbs 9.7g; Fat 3.1g; Protein 1.8g

Ingredients

3 parsnips, sliced
2 tsp olive oil
2 tsp cayenne pepper

1 tsp paprika
Salt and black pepper to taste

Directions

Place the slices into a bowl and sprinkle with oil, cayenne, paprika, salt and black pepper. Toss and arrange the fries in the basket.

Cook for 14 minutes at 360°F, giving it a toss halfway through cooking. Check to ensure they are golden and crispy.

Cilantro Roasted Eggplants

Total Time: 15 min | **Serves:** 6 | **Per serving:** Cal 95; Net Carbs 8.7 g; Fat 5.3g; Protein 2g

Ingredients

20 oz eggplants, sliced
1 tbsp olive oil

1 tsp cumin seeds
A handful of fresh cilantro

Directions

Preheat your Fryer to 350°F. In a bowl, mix oil, eggplants, and cumin. Stir to coat the eggplants well.

Place the carrots in your Air Fryer's cooking basket and cook for 12 minutes. Scatter fresh coriander over the carrots; serve and enjoy!

Sweet Baby Carrots

Total Time: 20 min | **Serves:** 4 | **Per serving:** Cal 54; Net Carbs 5g; Fat 5.8g; Protein 2.4g

Ingredients

1 pound baby carrots
1 tsp dried dill
1 tbsp olive oil

1 tbsp stevia
Salt and black pepper to taste

Directions

Preheat your Fryer to 350°F.

In a mixing bowl, mix oil, carrots and stevia. Gently stir to coat the carrots. Season with dill, pepper and salt. Place the carrots in your Air Fryer's basket and cook for 12 minutes.

Sweet & Spicy Nut Mix

Total Time: 25 min / **Serves:** 5 | **Per serving:** Cal 147; Net Carbs 10g; Fat 12g; Protein 3g

Ingredients

½ cup pecans
½ cup walnuts
½ cup almonds
A pinch cayenne pepper

2 tbsp stevia
2 tbsp egg whites
2 tsp cinnamon

Directions

Add the pepper, stevia, and cinnamon to a bowl and mix well; set aside. In another bowl, mix in the pecans, walnuts, almonds, and egg whites. Add the spice mixture to the nuts and give it a good mix. Lightly grease the fryer basket with cooking spray.

Pour in the nuts, and cook for 10 minutes. Stir the nuts using a wooden vessel, and cook for further for 10 minutes. Pour the nuts in the bowl. Let cool before crunching on them.

BRUNCH RECIPES

Veggie Cheese Quiche

Total Time: 50 min | **Serves**: 2 | **Per serving**: Cal 316; Net Carbs 1g; Fat 24g; Protein 10g

Ingredients

4 eggs
1 cup almond milk
2 medium broccoli, cut into florets
2 medium tomatoes, diced
4 medium carrots, diced

¼ cup feta cheese, crumbled
1 cup cheddar cheese, grated
Salt and black pepper to taste
1 tsp parsley, chopped
1 tsp dried thyme

Directions

Put the broccoli and carrots in a food steamer and cook until soft, about 10 minutes.

In a jug, crack in the eggs, add the parsley, salt, pepper, and thyme. Using a whisk, beat the eggs while adding the almond milk gradually until a pale mixture is attained.

Once the broccoli and carrots are ready, strain them through a sieve and set aside.

In a 3 X 3 cm quiche dish, add the carrots and broccoli. Put the tomatoes on top, then the feta and cheddar cheese following. Leave a little cheddar cheese. Pour the egg mixture over the layering and top with the remaining cheddar cheese.

Place the dish in the Air Fryer and cook at 350°F for 20 minutes. Once ready, remove the dish, use a knife to cut out slices, and serve.

Dijon Beet and Feta Salad

Total Time: 50 min | **Serves**: 4 | **Per serving**: Cal 225; Net Carbs 6.2g; Fat 16g; Protein 7g

Ingredients

4 large beets, stems trimmed
2 tbsp olive oil
Salt and pepper, to taste
3 tbsp red wine vinegar
¼ cup red onion, minced
2 cloves garlic, minced

1 ½ tbsp Dijon mustard
½ tbsp liquid stevia
1 tbsp fresh parsley, minced
½ tbsp fresh thyme leaves, minced
2 cups mixed baby lettuces
¾ cup feta cheese, crumbled

Directions

Preheat the Air Fryer to 390°F.

Place the beets on aluminum foil and drizzle with oil. Season with salt and pepper. Close up with aluminum foil the beets. Transfer to the Air Fryer and cook for 45 minutes. Remove and let cool.

In a bowl, mix red onion, garlic, mustard, vinegar and stevia. Whisk the ingredients until they are combined. Stir in the herbs and season with salt and pepper.

When the beets are chilled, cut them into slices of half an inch. Arrange on a platter, top with feta cheese, and scatter the dressing over. Garnish with baby lettuce and serve.

Classic French Toast Sticks

Total Time: 13 min | **Serves**: 3 | **Per serving**: Cal 165; Net Carbs 3.5g; Fat 13g; Protein 7.2g

Ingredients

5 slices low-carb bread
3 eggs
Salt and black pepper to taste
1 ½ tbsp butter

½ tsp cinnamon powder
A pinch nutmeg powder
A pinch clove powder

Directions

Preheat the Air Fryer to 350°F.

In a bowl, add the clove powder, eggs, nutmeg powder, and cinnamon powder. Beat well using a whisk. Season with salt and pepper.

Apply butter on both sides of the bread slices and cut them into 4 strips. Dip each strip in the egg mixture and arrange in one layer in the fryer basket. Cook for 2 minutes.

Once ready, pull out the fryer basket and spray the toasts with cooking spray. Flip the toasts and spray the other side with cooking spray.

Slide the fryer basket back into the Air Fryer and continue cooking for 4 minutes. Keep a constant eye on the toasts to prevent them from burning.

Once the toasts are golden brown, remove them onto a serving platter.

Dust with cinnamon and serve.

Hot Egg Avocado Salad

Total Time: 7 min | **Serves:** 3 | **Per serving:** Cal 472; Net Carbs 4.2g; Fat 41g; Protein 17g;

Ingredients

6 cooked eggs
2 avocados, peeled and chopped
2 cups tomatoes, chopped
½ cup red onion, chopped
Salt and black pepper, to taste

2 tbsp keto mayo
2 tbsp sour cream
1 tbsp lemon juice
6 drops hot sauce

Directions

In the basket of the Air Fryer, place thinly sliced eggs. Add the tomatoes, the red onion, salt, and pepper. Set the timer to 7 minutes and the heat to 340°F.

When ready, transfer the ingredients into a bowl. Stir in the mayo, the sour cream, the lemon juice, and the hot sauce. Garnish with avocado.

Crispy Hash Browns

Total Time: 45 min | **Serves:** 3 | **Per serving**: Cal 312; Net Carbs 1.6g; Fat 15g; Protein 16g

Ingredients

7 radishes, shredded
Salt and black pepper to taste
1 tsp garlic powder
1 tsp chili flakes

1 tsp onion powder
1 egg, beaten
1 tbsp olive oil

Directions

Place a skillet over medium heat on a stove top, add the olive oil and radishes. Sauté until turn evenly golden, about 7-8 minutes. Transfer to a bowl and let them cool completely.

After they have cooled, add in the egg, pepper, salt, chili flakes, onion powder, and garlic powder. Mix well.

In a flat plate, spread the mixture and pat firmly with your fingers. Refrigerate for 20 minutes and preheat the Air Fryer to 350°F. Remove from the fridge and use a knife to divide it into equal sizes.

Grease the basket of the Air Fryer with cooking spray and place the patties in the basket.

Close the Air Fryer and cook them at 350°F for 15 minutes. Open the Air Fryer and turn the hash browns with a spatula. Cook further for 6 minutes. Serve with sunshine eggs.

Buttered Egg in Hole

Total Time: 11 min | **Serves**: 2 | **Per serving**: Cal 220; Net Carbs 1g; Fat 16g; Protein 8g

Ingredients

2 slices low-carb bread
2 eggs

Salt and black pepper to taste
2 tbsp butter

Directions

Place a 3 X 3 cm heatproof bowl in the fryer basket and brush with butter.

Make a hole in the middle of the bread slices with a bread knife and place in the heatproof bowl in 2 batches. Break an egg into the center of each hole. Season with salt and pepper. Close the Air Fryer and cook for 4 minutes at 330°F. Turn the bread with a spatula and cook for another 4 minutes.

Almond Blueberry Tart

Total Time: 40 min | **Serves**: 10 | **Per serving**: Cal 210; Net Carbs 10.2g; Fat 16g; Protein 3.4g

Ingredients

½ cup ground almonds
3 ½ cups almond flour
1 tsp baking powder
1 tsp ground cinnamon
3 eggs, lightly beaten

½ cup coconut oil
⅓ cup almond milk
2 tsp vanilla extract
2 cups blueberries

Directions

Spray a baking pan that fits in your air fryer with cooking spray.

In a bowl, add almonds, almond flour, baking powder and cinnamon into and stir well.

In another bowl, whisk eggs, oil, almond milk and vanilla. Stir the wet ingredients gently into the oat mixture. Fold in the blueberries.

Pour the mixture in the pan and place in the fryer. Cook for 30 minutes at 330°F.

When ready, check if the bars are nice and soft.

Breakfast Sausage & Egg Casserole

Total Time: 20 min | **Serves**: 6 | **Per serving**: Cal 494; Net Carbs 5.3g; Fat 41g; Protein 26g

Ingredients

1 lb breakfast sausage, minced
6 eggs
2 tbsp olive oil
1 red pepper, diced
1 green pepper, diced

1 yellow pepper, diced
1 onion, diced
2 cups cheddar cheese, shredded
Salt and black pepper to taste
Fresh parsley to garnish

Directions

Warm olive oil in a skillet over medium heat, add the sausage and cook until brown, stirring occasionally. Once done, drain any excess fat derived from cooking; set aside.

Arrange the sausage on the bottom of a greased casserole dish. Top with onion, red pepper, green pepper, and yellow pepper. Spread the cheese on top.

Beat the eggs and season with salt and black pepper. Pour the mixture over the casserole.

Place the casserole dish in the fryer basket, close the Air Fryer and bake at 355°F for 13-15 minutes. Serve warm garnished with fresh parsley.

Keto Pumpkin Seed Brown Bread

Total Time: 28 min | **Serves:** 4 | **Per serving:** Cal 396; Net Carbs 2.8g; Fat 36g; Protein 13g

Ingredients

8 oz almond flour
1 oz liquid stevia
3 oz water

1 egg
2 tbsp butter

Directions

Combine flour, stevia, and water. Keep mixing the components with hands.

Add the butter and knead the mixture very well. Let bread dough rest, keep warm and covered, for about 2 hours until it grows in size.

Then, divide the dough into small balls of 1 oz each and place in the baking paper. Brush the balls with the egg. Let the dough rest again for 30-40 minutes. Place dough balls in a tray. Cook in the Air Fryer at 330°F, until brown and crispy.

Vanilla Coconut Scones

Total Time: 30 min | **Serves:** 4 | **Per serving:** Cal 167; Net Carbs 4.2g; Fat 15.4g; Protein 3.4g

Ingredients

2 cups almond flour
⅓ cup stevia
2 tsp baking powder
½ cup almonds, sliced
¾ cup coconut, shredded

¼ cup cold butter, cut into cubes
½ cup almond milk
1 egg
1 tsp vanilla extract

Directions

Line air fryer basket with baking paper. Mix together almond flour, stevia, baking powder, almonds and coconut. Rub the butter into the dry ingredients with hands to form a sandy, crumbly texture.

Whisk together egg, almond milk and vanilla extract. Pour into the dry ingredients and stir to combine.

Sprinkle a working board with almond flour, lay the dough onto the board and give it a few kneads. Shape into a rectangle and cut into 9 squares.

Arrange the squares in the air fryer's basket and cook for 14 minutes at 390°F. Serve immediately.

Steamed Asparagus Omelet

Total Time: 8 min | **Serves:** 2 | **Per serving:** Cal 287; Net Carbs 2g; Fat 23g; Protein 15g

Ingredients

3 eggs
1 tbsp Parmesan cheese
2 tbsp warm water

A pinch of salt
A pinch of black pepper
5 steamed asparagus tips

Directions

Start by whisking the eggs, cheese, water, salt, and pepper in a large bowl, then blend them. Spray a pan with cooking spray and steam. Add to the Air Fryer basket.

Pour the egg mixture into the basket and add the asparagus. Set the temperature to 320°F and cook for 5 minutes.

Spinach & Ham Eggs

Total Time: 8 min | **Serves:** 3 | **Per serving:** Cal 223; Net Carbs 3.1g; Fat 13g; Protein 18g

Ingredients

1 lb spinach
4 oz sliced ham
4 eggs

1 tbsp olive oil
4 tbsp water
Salt and black pepper, to taste

Directions

Preheat the Air Fryer to 360°F. Butter 4 ramekins.

In each ramekin, place the spinach, one egg, an ounce of ham, a tablespoon of water, salt, and pepper. Line the ramekins in the Air Fryer's basket. Set the timer to 10 minutes (6-7 minutes for runny eggs).

Modern Pumpkin Pie French Toast

Total Time: 26 min | **Serves:** 4 | **Per serving:** Cal 267; Net Carbs 3.2g; Fat 19g; Protein 8g

Ingredients

2 large eggs, beaten
¼ cup water
¼ cup pumpkin purée

¼ tsp pumpkin pie spices
4 slices low-carb bread
¼ cup butter

Directions

In a large bowl, mix the eggs, the water, the pumpkin, and the pie spice. Whisk until you obtain a smooth mixture. Dip both sides of the bread in the egg mixture.

Place the rack inside the Air Fryer's cooking basket. Set the temperature to 340°F and set time to 10 minutes. Serve the pumpkin pie with butter.

Buttered Scrambled Eggs

Total Time: 6 min | **Serves:** 1 | **Per serving:** Cal 180; Net Carbs 0.2g; Fat 14g; Protein 11g

Ingredients

2 eggs
¼ oz butter, melted

Salt and black pepper to taste

Directions

Break and whisk the eggs. Preheat the Air Fryer to 240°F. Add butter to Air Fryer's basket, and place the eggs. Cook for 6 minutes. Serve the eggs with cheese and tomatoes.

Roasted Cabbage Salad

Total Time: 30 min | **Serves:** 3 | **Per serving:** Cal 145; Net Carbs 5.2g; Fat 10g; Protein 3g

Ingredients

2 tbsp olive oil
½ head green cabbage cut into 4 wedges
A pinch of garlic powder

A pinch of red pepper flakes
2 small halved lemons

Directions

Preheat the Air Fryer to 390°F.

Brush the sides of each of the cabbage wedges with the olive oil. Sprinkle with garlic powder and add a pinch of red pepper flakes and salt. Roast the cabbage wedges in the Air Fryer for 30 minutes.

Make sure to flip them at least once. Squeeze lemon juice and enjoy its delicious taste!

Balsamic Radish and Mozzarella Salad

Total Time: 35 min | **Serves:** 4 | **Per serving:** Cal 235; Net Carbs 2.6g; Fat 15g; Protein 19g

Ingredients

1 lb radishes with their tops
2 tbsp olive oil
1 tsp salt

½ tsp ground black pepper
½ lb mozzarella cheese
2 tbsp balsamic vinegar

Directions

Rinse and pat dry the radishes using a paper towel. Make sure to trim the wilted stems from the radish.

In a large bowl, place the radishes and drizzle with oil, a pinch of salt and a pinch of pepper. Transfer the ingredients to the Air Fryer. Set the heat to 350°F and the timer to 35 minutes.

Once cooked, drizzle with balsamic vinegar and top with the cheese to serve.

Yellow Bell Peppers & Asparagus Salad

Total Time: 10 min | **Serves:** 3 | **Per serving:** Cal 232; Net Carbs 6.2g; Fat 16g; Protein 10g

Ingredients

1 lb asparagus, trimmed and cubed
2 yellow bell peppers, cut and cubed
¼ cup almonds, toasted
½ cup Parmesan cheese, grated
2 tbsp olive oil

2 tbsp Dijon mustard
2 cloves garlic, minced
2 tbsp lime juice
1 tbsp hot sauce

Directions

Preheat the Air Fryer to 390°F.

Mix the asparagus and the bell peppers with 1 tbsp of olive oil. Cook them for 10 minutes in the Air Fryer Remove from the heat and add the almonds and the parmesan cheese.

In another bowl, mix 1 tbsp of olive oil, the mustard, the garlic, the lime juice, and the hot sauce. Combine the 2 groups ofFood and serve.

Sausage Thai Omelet

Total Time: 20 min | **Serves:** 3 | **Per serving:** Cal 253; Net Carbs 2.2g; Fat 11g; Protein 11g

Ingredients

4 eggs
2 tbsp fish sauce
2 tbsp white pepper powder
Juice from ½ lime
2 cloves garlic, minced

1 minced shallot
½ cup sausage, finely cut
1 handful fresh spinach
1 fresh green onion, chopped
Cilantro, chopped to garnish

Directions

Heat oil in a pan. Crack the eggs into a large bowl. Add the fish sauce and the pepper.

Whisk until bubbles start to appear in the mixture. Add the remaining ingredients and keep whisking until well combined.

Pour the obtained mixture inside the pan and place it in the basket of the Air Fryer.

Cook for 10 minutes at 340°F. Sprinkle with cilantro to serve.

Traditional English Toast

Total Time: 15 min | **Serves:** 3 | **Per serving:** Cal 245; Net Carbs 7.2g; Fat 10.5g; Protein 11g

Ingredients

6 slices zero carb bread
2 eggs
¼ cup heavy cream

⅓ cup powdered erythritol mixed with 1 tsp ground cinnamon
6 tbsp sugar-free caramel topping

Directions

In a bowl, whisk eggs and cream. Dip each piece of bread into the egg and cream. Dip the bread into the cinnamon mixture until well-coated.

On a clean board, lay the coated slices and spread three of the slices with about 2 tbsp of caramel topping each, around the center. Place the remaining three slices on top to form three sandwiches.

Spray the air fryer basket with cooking spray. Arrange the sandwiches into the fryer and cook for 10 minutes at 340°F, turning once halfway through cooking.

Nut Choco Muffins

Total Time: 40 min | **Serves:** 6 | **Per serving:** Cal 306; Net Carbs 7.2g; Fat 32g; Protein 6g

Ingredients

½ cup butter, melted
½ cup powdered erythritol
2 eggs, lightly beaten
1 cup strawberries, mashed
1 tsp vanilla extract
2 cups almond flour

1 tsp baking powder
½ tsp baking soda
1 tsp ground cinnamon
½ cup hazelnuts, chopped
½ cup dark chocolate chips, unsweetened

Directions

Spray 10-hole muffin with cooking spray.

In a bowl, whisk butter, erythritol, eggs, strawberries and vanilla, until well-combine. Sift in almond flour, baking powder, baking soda and cinnamon without overmixing.

Stir in the hazelnuts and chocolate. Pour the mixture into the muffin holes and place in the air fryer. Cook for 30 minutes at 350°F, checking at the around 20-minute mark.

Almond Raspberry Pancakes

Total Time: 15 min | **Serves:** 4 | **Per serving:** Cal 483; Net Carbs 10.8 g; Fat 15.6g; Protein 17g

Ingredients

2 cups almond flour
1 cup almond milk
3 eggs, beaten
1 tsp baking powder
1 cup erythritol, powdered

1 ½ tsp vanilla extract
½ cup frozen raspberries, thawed
2 tbsp liquid stevia
Pinch of salt

Directions

Preheat the air fryer to 390°F.

In a bowl, mix the almond flour, baking powder, salt, almond milk, eggs, vanilla extract, stevia, and erythritol until smooth. Stir in the raspberries. Do it gently to avoid coloring the batter.

Grease a baking dish with cooking spray. Drop the batter onto the dish. Just make sure to leave some space between the pancakes. If there is some batter left; repeat the process. Cook for 10 minutes.

Mozzarella & Ham Sandwiches

Total Time: 25 min | **Serves:** 2 | **Per serving:** Cal 275; Net Carbs 6.2g; Fat 13g; Protein 18g

Ingredients

4 slices zero carb bread
2 tbsp mayonnaise
2 slices ham
2 lettuce leaves

1 tomato, sliced
2 slices mozzarella cheese
Salt and black pepper to taste

Directions

On a clean board, lay the zero carb bread slices and spread with mayonnaise.

Top 2 of the slices with ham, lettuce, tomato and mozzarella. Season with salt and pepper. Top with the remaining two slices to form two sandwiches. Spray with cooking spray and transfer to the air fryer.

Cook for 14 minutes at 340°F, flipping once halfway through cooking. Serve hot!

Grandma's Zucchini Cakes

Total Time: 20 min | **Serves:** 4 | **Per serving:** Cal 357; Net Carbs 7.6g; Fat 25g; Protein 18g

Ingredients

1 ½ cups almond flour
1 tsp cinnamon
3 eggs
2 tsp baking powder
2 tbsp stevia
1 cup almond milk

2 tbsp butter, melted
1 tbsp yogurt
½ cup zucchini, shredded
Pinch of salt
2 tbsp cream cheese

Directions

Preheat the air fryer to 350°F. In a bowl, whisk the eggs along with the stevia, salt, cinnamon, cream cheese, almond flour, and baking powder.

In another bowl, combine all liquid ingredients. Combine dry and liquid mixtures; stir in zucchini.

Line the muffin tins and pour the batter into the tins. Cook for 12 minutes. Check with a toothpick. You may need to cook them for an additional 2 to 3 minutes.

Mediterranean Quiche

Total Time: 40 min | **Serves:** 2 | **Per serving:** Cal 540; Net Carbs 7.4g; Fat 44g; Protein 25.8g

Ingredients

4 eggs
½ cup chopped tomatoes
1 cup feta cheese, crumbled
1 tbsp basil, chopped
1 tbsp oregano, chopped

¼ cup kalamata olives, chopped
¼ cup onion, chopped
2 tbsp olive oil
½ cup almond milk
Salt and black pepper to taste

Directions

Preheat the air fryer to 340°F. Brush a pie pan with the olive oil.

Beat the eggs along with the almond milk and some salt and pepper.

Stir in all of the remaining ingredients. Pour the egg mixture into the pan. Cook for 30 minutes.

Welsh-Style Rarebit

Total Time: 15 min | **Serves:** 2 | **Per serving:** Cal 405; Net Carbs 4.5g; Fat 27g; Protein 26g

Ingredients

3 slices zero carbs bread
1 tsp smoked paprika
2 eggs

1 tsp Dijon mustard
4 ½ oz cheddar cheese , grated
Salt and black pepper to taste

Directions

Toast the bread in the air fryer to your liking.

Whisk the eggs. Stir in the mustard, cheddar and paprika. Season with salt and pepper.

Spread the mixture on the toasts. Cook the bread slices for about 10 minutes at 360°F.

Bacon & Chives Egg Cups

Total Time: 30 min | **Serves:** 10 | **Per serving:** Cal 245; Net Carbs 1.5g; Fat 21g; Protein 14g

Ingredients

10 eggs, lightly beaten
10 bacon rashers, cut into small pieces
½ cup chives, chopped

1 brown onion, chopped
1 cup cheddar cheese, grated
Salt and black pepper to taste

Directions

Spray a 10-hole muffin pan with cooking spray. In a bowl, add eggs, bacon, chives, onion, cheese, salt and pepper, and stir to combine. Pour into muffin pans and place inside the fryer. Cook for 12 minutes at 330°F, until nice and set.

Tuscan Omelet

Total Time: 10 min | **Serves:** 2 | **Per serving:** Cal 328; Net Carbs 6.2g; Fat 24g; Protein 21g

Ingredients

4 eggs, lightly beaten
2 tbsp heavy cream
2 cups spinach, chopped
1 cup mushrooms, chopped

3 oz feta cheese, crumbled
A handful of fresh parsley, chopped
Salt and black pepper to taste

Directions

Spray your air fryer basket with oil spray.

In a bowl, whisk eggs and until combined. Stir in spinach, mushrooms, feta, parsley, salt and pepper.

Pour into the basket and cook for 6 minutes at 350°F. Serve immediately with a touch of tangy tomato relish.

Basil & Kale Omelet

Total Time: 15 min | **Serves**: 1 | **Per serving:** Cal 294; Net Carbs 3.9g; Fat 19.5g; Protein 24.7 g

Ingredients

3 eggs
3 tbsp cottage cheese
3 tbsp kale, chopped
½ tbsp basil, chopped

½ tbsp parsley, chopped
Salt and black pepper to taste
1 tsp olive oil

Directions

Add oil to the air fryer and preheat it to 330°F.

Beat the eggs with some salt and pepper, in a bowl. Stir in the rest of the ingredients. Pour the mixture into the air fryer and bake for 10 minutes.

Green Onion & Cheese Omelet

Total Time: 15 min | **Serves**: 1 | **Per serving:** Cal 347.3; Net Carbs 6 g; Fat 23.2 g; Protein 13g

Ingredients

2 eggs
2 tbsp cheddar cheese, grated
1 tsp soy sauce, sugar-free

1 green onion, sliced
¼ tsp pepper
1 tbsp olive oil

Directions

Whisk the eggs along with the pepper and soy sauce.

Preheat the air fryer to 350°F. Heat the olive oil and add the egg mixture and the onion. Cook for 8 to 10 minutes. Top with the grated cheddar cheese.

Morning Muffins

Total Time: 15 min | **Serves:** 4 | **Per serving:** Cal 214; Net Carbs 6.3g; Fat 17g; Protein 3g

Ingredients

1 ¼ cup almond flour
¼ cup mashed strawberries
¼ cup powdered erythritol
1 tsp almond milk

1 tbsp walnuts, chopped
½ tsp baking powder
¼ cup butter, room temperature

Directions

Preheat the air fryer to 320°F. Place the erythritol, walnuts, strawberries, and butter in a bowl; mix to combine. In another bowl, combine the almond flour and baking powder.

Combine the two mixtures together and stir in the milk. Grease a muffin tin and pour the batter in. Bake in your air fryer for 10 minutes.

Cheesy Parsnip & Spinach Frittata

Total Time: 35 min | **Serves:** 4 | **Per serving:** Cal 235; Net Carbs 8.2g; Fat 9.5g; Protein 17.4g

Ingredients

2 cups parsnip cubes, boiled, soft
2 cups spinach, chopped
5 eggs, lightly beaten
¼ cup heavy cream

1 cup mozzarella cheese, grated
½ cup parsley, chopped
Fresh thyme, chopped
Salt and black pepper to taste

Directions

Spray the air fryer's basket with oil. Arrange the parsnip cubes inside. Whisk eggs, cream, spinach, mozzarella, parsley, thyme, salt and pepper, and pour over the potatoes. Cook for 16 minutes at 400°F, until nice and golden.

Speedy Grilled Cheese

Total Time: 10 min | **Serves:** 1 | **Per serving:** Cal 452; Net Carbs 2.3g; Fat 32g; Protein 17g

Ingredients

2 tsp butter
2 slices zero carb bread

3 slices American cheese

Directions

Preheat the air fryer to 370°F. Spread 1 tsp of butter on the outside of each of the bread. Place the cheese on the inside of one bread slice. Top with the other slice. Cook for 4 minutes. Flip the sandwich over and cook for 4 more minutes. Serve cut diagonally.

Feta Frittata with Chorizo Sausage

Total Time: 12 min | **Serves:** 2 | **Per serving:** Cal 354; Net Carbs 7.4 g; Fat 22g; Protein 20g

Ingredients

3 eggs
1 large turnip, boiled and cubed
½ cup feta cheese , crumbled
1 tbsp parsley, chopped

½ chorizo sausage, sliced
3 tbsp olive oil
Salt and black pepper to taste

Directions

Pour the olive oil into the air fryer and preheat it to 330°F. Cook the chorizo just so it becomes slightly browned. Beat the eggs with some salt and pepper in a bowl. Stir in all of the remaining ingredients. Pour the mixture into the air fryer and cook for 6 minutes.

Prosciutto, Mozzarella & Egg Cakes

Total Time: 20 min | **Serves:** 2 | **Per serving:** Cal 291; Net Carbs 5.9g; Fat 20.5g; Protein13g

Ingredients

2 slices zero carbs bread
2 prosciutto slices, chopped
2 eggs
4 tomato slices
¼ tsp balsamic vinegar

2 tbsp grated mozzarella cheese
¼ tsp stevia
2 tbsp mayonnaise
Salt and black pepper to taste

Directions

Preheat the air fryer to 320 degrees.

Grease 2 ramekins. Place one bread slice in the bottom of each ramekin. Arrange 2 tomato slices on top. Divide the mozzarella between the ramekins. Crack the eggs over the mozzarella. Drizzle with stevia and balsamic vinegar. Season with salt and pepper. Cook for 10 minutes, or until desired. Top with mayonnaise.

BEEF AND LAMB RECIPES

Tasty Beef Cauli Rice

Total Time: 37 min | **Serves:** 2 | **Per serving:** Cal 445; Net Carbs 5.2g; Fat 21g; Protein 49g

Ingredients

Beef:

1 lb beef steak

Salt and black pepper to taste

Cauli rice:

2 ½ cups cauli rice

1 ½ tbsp soy sauce, sugar-free

2 tsp sesame oil

2 tsp ginger, minced

2 tsp vinegar

1 clove garlic, minced

¼ cup chopped broccoli

¼ cup green beans

Directions

Put the beef on a chopping board and use a knife to cut it in 2-inch strips.

Add the beef to a bowl, sprinkle with pepper and salt, and mix it with a spoon.

Let sit for 10 minutes.

Preheat the Air Fryer to 400°F.

Add the beef to the fryer basket, and cook for 5 minutes.

Turn the beef strips with kitchen tongs and cook further for 3 minutes.

Once ready, remove the beef into a safe oven dish that fits into the fryer basket.

Add the cauli rice, broccoli, green beans, garlic, ginger, sesame oil, vinegar and soy sauce. Mix evenly using a spoon.

Place the dish in the fryer basket carefully, close the Air Fryer and cook at 370°F for 10 minutes.

Open the Air Fryer, mix the rice well, and cook further for 4 minutes. Season with salt and pepper as desired.

Dish the cauli fried rice into a serving bowl.

Serve with hot sauce.

Homemade Worcestershire Beef Burgers

Total Time: 25 min | **Serves**: 4 | **Per serving**: Cal 421; Net Carbs 3.2g; Fat 39g; Protein 21g

Ingredients

1 ½ lb ground beef
Salt and black pepper to taste
¼ tsp liquid smoke
2 tsp onion powder
1 tsp garlic powder

1 ½ tbsp Worcestershire sauce
8 lettuce leaves
4 tbsp mayonnaise
1 large tomato, sliced
4 slices cheddar cheese

Directions

Preheat the Air Fryer to 370°F.

In a mixing bowl, combine the ground beef, salt, black pepper, liquid smoke, onion powder, garlic powder and Worcestershire sauce using your hands. Form 4 patties out of the mixture.

Place the patties in the fryer basket making sure to leave enough space between them. Ideally, work with two patties at a time. Close the Air Fryer and cook for 10 minutes.

Turn the beef with kitchen tongs, reduce the temperature to 350°F, and cook further for 5 minutes. Remove the patties onto a plate.

Assemble burgers with the lettuce, mayonnaise, sliced cheese, and sliced tomato.

Paprika Beef Ribs

Total Time: 65 min | **Serves**: 6 | **Per serving**: Cal 561; Net Carbs 3.15g; Fat 53g; Protein 28g

Ingredients

2 racks beef ribs
2 tbsp fresh ginger, ground
Salt and black pepper to taste

5 drops liquid stevia
1 tbsp Spanish paprika

Directions

Mix the seasonings very well. Coat each side of the beef ribs.

Arrange the ribs in a preheated Air Fryer basket.

Set the heat to 390°F and the timer to 55 minutes. Top with the seasonings.

Simple Roast Beef with Herbs

Total Time: 60 min | **Serves**: 2 | **Per serving**: Cal 358; Net Carbs 2g; Fat 24.6g; Protein 26.4g

Ingredients

2 tsp olive oil
1 lb beef roast
½ tsp dried rosemary

½ tsp dried thyme
½ tsp dried oregano
Salt and black pepper to taste

Directions

Preheat the Air Fryer to 400°F.

Drizzle the oil on the beef and sprinkle the salt, pepper, and herbs. Rub into the meat.

Place the meat in the fryer basket and cook it for 45 minutes for medium-rare and 50 minutes for well done. Check halfway through and flip to ensure they cook evenly.

Wrap the beef in foil for 10 minutes after cooking to allow the juices to reabsorb into the meat. Slice the meat using a knife and serve with a side of steamed asparagus.

Saucy Beef Tenderloin

Total Time: 40 min | **Serves**: 3 | **Per serving**: Cal 235; Net Carbs 4g; Fat 11g; Protein 18g

Ingredients

Beef:
2 lb beef tenderloin, cut into strips
Sauce:

½ cup almond flour

1 tbsp minced ginger
1 tbsp minced garlic
½ cup chopped green onions
2 tbsp olive oil
½ cup soy sauce, sugar-free
½ cup water

¼ cup vinegar
¼ cup erythritol
1 tsp arrowroot starch
½ tsp red chili flakes
Salt and black pepper to taste

Directions

Pour the almond flour in a bowl, add the beef strips and dredge them in the flour. Spray the fryer basket with cooking spray and arrange the beef strips in it. Spray with cooking spray.

Cook the beef at 400°F in the Air Fryer for 4 minutes. Slide out and shake the fryer basket to toss the beef strips. Cook further for 3 minutes. Set aside.

To make the sauce, pour the arrowroot starch in a bowl and mix it with 3 to 4 teaspoons of water until well dissolved. Set aside.

Place a wok or saucepan over medium heat on a stove top and add the olive oil, garlic, and ginger. Stir continually for 10 seconds.

Add the soy sauce, vinegar, and remaining water. Stir well and bring to boil for 2 minutes. Stir in the erythritol, chili flakes, and arrowroot starch mixture. Add the beef strips, stir and cook for 3 minutes. Stir in the green onions and cook for 2 minutes. Season with pepper and salt as desired. Turn off the heat.

Beef Meatloaf with Tomato-Basil Sauce

Total Time: 40 min | **Serves**: 5 | **Per serving**: Cal 260; Net Carbs 1g; Fat 13g; Protein 26g

Ingredients

1 cup sugar-free tomato basil sauce
1 ½ lb ground beef
1 ¼ cup onion, diced
2 tbsp minced garlic
2 tbsp minced ginger
½ cup pork rinds, crushed

½ cup Parmesan cheese, grated
Salt and black pepper to season
2 tsp cayenne pepper
½ tsp dried basil
⅓ cup parsley, chopped
2 egg whites

Directions

Preheat the Air Fryer to 360°F.

In a mixing bowl, add the beef, half of the tomato sauce, onion, garlic, ginger, pork rinds, cheese, salt, pepper, cayenne pepper, dried basil, parsley, and egg whites. Mix well.

Grease an 8 or 10-inch pan with cooking spray and scoop the meat mixture into it. The container should fit into the Air Fryer otherwise use a smaller size. With a spatula, shape the meat into the pan while pressing firmly. Use a brush to apply the remaining tomato sauce on the meat. Place the pan in the fryer basket and close the Air Fryer.

Cook for 25 minutes. After 15 minutes, open the Air Fryer and use a meat thermometer to ensure the meat has reached 160 F internally. Otherwise cook further for 5 minutes.

Remove the pan, drain any excess liquid and fat. Let meatloaf cool for 20 minutes before slicing. Serve with a side of sautéed green beans.

Holiday Beef Veggie Mix with Hoisin Sauce

Total Time: 55 min | **Serves**: 6 | **Per serving**: Cal 428; Net Carbs 8.7g; Fat 25.5g; Protein 37.8g

Ingredients

Hoisin sauce:

2 tbsp soy sauce, sugar-free

1 tbsp peanut butter

½ tsp sriracha hot sauce

1 tsp stevia sweetener

1 tsp vinegar

3 cloves garlic, minced

Beef veggie mix:

2 lb beef sirloin, cut in strips

2 yellow peppers, cut in strips

2 green peppers, cut in strips

2 green peppers, cut in strips

2 medium white onions, cut in strips

1 medium red onions, cut in strips

1 lb broccoli, cut in florets

2 tbsp soy sauce, sugar-free

2 tsp sesame oil

3 tsp minced garlic

2 tsp ground ginger

½ cup water

1 tbsp olive oil

Directions

To make the sauce: in a pan, add the soy sauce, peanut butter, stevia sweetener, hot sauce, rice vinegar, and minced garlic.

Bring it to simmer over low heat until reduced, about 15 minutes. Stir occasionally using a vessel and let it cool.

For the veggie mix: add to the chilled hoisin sauce, minced garlic, sesame oil, soy sauce, ground ginger, and water. Mix well. Add the meat, mix with a spoon, and place it in the refrigerator to marinate for 20 minutes.

Meanwhile, add the broccoli florets, the peppers, onions, and olive oil to a bowl, mix to coat well.

Pour the veggies in the fryer basket and cook for 5 minutes at 400 degrees F.

Open the Air Fryer, stir the veggies, and cook further for 5 minutes if they are not softened. Remove the veggies to a serving plate and set aside.

Remove the meat from the fridge and drain the liquid into a small bowl. Add the beef into the fryer basket, close the Air Fryer, and cook at 380°F for 8 minutes.

Slide out the fryer basket and shake it to toss the beef strips. Cook for 7 minutes. Transfer the beef strips to the veggie plate. Pour the cooking sauce over and serve.

Beef Sausage & Mozzarella Omelet

Total Time: 20 min | **Serves**: 2 | **Per serving:** Cal 590; Net Carbs 6g; Fat 42.5g; Protein 44g

Ingredients

1 beef sausage, chopped
4 slices prosciutto, chopped
3 oz salami, chopped
1 cup mozzarella cheese, grated

4 eggs
1 tbsp onion, chopped
1 tbsp ketchup, sugar-free

Directions

Preheat the air fryer to 350°F.

Whisk the eggs with the ketchup in a bowl. Stir in the onion. Brown the sausage in the air fryer for about 2 minutes.

Meanwhile, combine the egg mixture, mozzarella cheese, salami and prosciutto. Pour the egg mixture over the sausage and give it a stir. Cook for about 10 minutes.

Spiced Rib Eye Steak with Avocado Salsa

Total Time: 32 min | **Serves**: 4 | **Per serving**: Cal 523; Net Carbs 2.3g; Fat 45g; Protein 32g

Ingredients

1 ½ lb rib eye steak
2 tsp olive oil
1 tbsp chipotle chili pepper

Salt and black pepper to taste
1 avocado, diced
Juice from ½ lime

Directions

Place the steak on a chopping board. Pour the olive oil over and sprinkle with the chipotle pepper, salt, and black pepper. Rub the spices on the meat. Leave to sit and marinate for 10 minutes.

Preheat the Air Fryer to 400°F.

Pull out the fryer basket and place the meat in it. Slide it back into the Air Fryer and cook for 14 minutes. Turn the steak and continue cooking for 6 minutes. Remove the steak, cover with foil, and let it sit for 5 minutes before slicing.

Mash the avocado with potato mash. Add in the lime juice and mix until smooth. Taste, adjust the seasoning. Slice and serve the steak with salsa.

Stuffed Savoy Cabbage Rolls

Total Time: 35 min | **Serves**: 4 | **Per serving**: Cal 317; Net Carbs 2.1g; Fat 21.2g; Protein 27.2g

Ingredients

½ lb ground beef
8 savoy cabbage leaves
1 small onion, chopped
¼ packet taco seasoning
1 tbsp cilantro lime rotel

½ cup shredded Mexican cheese
2 tsp olive oil
Salt and black pepper to taste
2 cloves garlic, minced
1 tsp chopped cilantro

Directions

Preheat the Air Fryer to 400°F.

Grease a skillet with cooking spray and place it over medium heat on a stove top. Add the onions and garlic. Sauté until fragrant.

Add the beef, pepper, salt, and taco seasoning. Cook until the beef browns while breaking the meat with a vessel as it cooks. Add the cilantro Rotel and stir well to combine.

Lay 4 of the savoy cabbage leaves on a flat surface and scoop the beef mixture in the center of them and sprinkle with the Mexican cheese.

Wrap them diagonally and double wrap them with the remaining 4 cabbage leaves. Arrange the 4 rolls in the fryer basket and spray with cooking spray.

Close the Air Fryer and cook for 8 minutes. Flip the rolls, spray with cooking spray, and continue cooking for 4 minutes. Remove, garnish with cilantro and allow them to cool. Serve with cheese dip.

Sweet & Spicy Veggie Beef

Total Time: 25 min | **Serves:** 4 | **Per serving:** Cal 235; Net Carbs 6.2g; Fat 11g; Protein 27g

Ingredients

2 beef steaks, sliced into thin strips
2 garlic cloves, chopped
2 tsp stevia
1 tsp oyster sauce
1 tsp cayenne pepper
½ tsp olive oil

Juice of 1 lime
Salt and black pepper to taste
1 cauliflower, cut into florets
2 carrots, cut into chunks
1 cup green beans

Directions

In a bowl, add beef, garlic, stevia, oyster sauce, cayenne, oil, lime juice, salt and black pepper, and stir to combine.

Place the beef along with the garlic and some of the juices into your air fryer and top with the veggies. Cook on 400°F for 8 minutes, turning once halfway through cooking.

Lime Marinated Beef Fajitas

Total Time: 15 min | **Serves:** 4 | **Per serving:** Cal 567; Net Carbs 2.1g; Fat 46g; Protein 41g

Ingredients

2 lb beef, cut into thin strips
6 tbsp coconut oil
½ cup lime juice
4 garlic cloves, mashed
½ tbsp chili powder
1 red bell pepper, chopped
1 hot pepper, sliced
2 onions, sliced
12 flaxseed tortillas
2 tbsp butter, melted
1 avocado, sliced

Directions

Prepare a combination of oil and lime juice. Add the spices and the beef and mix the ingredients very well. Marinate for 5 hours.

Remove the marinated mixture from the fridge and pat dry the meat.

Take the basket of the Air Fryer and arrange the meat portions inside.

Pour 2 tbsp of olive oil over the meat. Set the timer to 35 minutes and the heat to 360°F.

In the meantime, sauté the vegetables in the coconut oil and then add them to the Air Fryer.

Heat the tortillas for a short time in a non-stick pan and brush them with melted butter.

Serve the beef meat with the tortillas and avocado slices.

Butter Beef Schnitzel with Lemon

Total Time: 25 min | **Serves:** 4 | **Per serving:** Cal 675; Net Carbs 1.9g; Fat 37g; Protein 73g

Ingredients

4 beef schnitzel cutlets
½ cup almond flour
2 eggs, beaten
Salt and black pepper to taste

1 cup pork rinds, crushed
1 lemon, sliced
½ stick butter, sliced

Directions

Coat the cutlets in almond flour and shake off any excess. Dip the coated cutlets into the beaten egg. Sprinkle with salt and black pepper.

Then dip into the pork rinds and to coat well. Spray them generously with oil and cook for 10 minutes at 360°F, turning once halfway through cooking. Serve topped with a slice of butter and lemon.

Mustard Lamb with Pumpkin

Total Time: 35 min | **Serves:** 2 | **Per serving:** Cal 587; Net Carbs 3.2g; Fat 39g; Protein 46g

Ingredients

1 lb lamb rack
1 tbsp Dijon mustard
2 oz pork rinds, crushed
2 tbsp fresh herbs, chopped
1 oz Parmesan cheese, grated

1 lemon zest
1 tbsp olive oil.
1 medium pumpkin
1 tbsp olive oil
Salt and black pepper to taste

Directions

Preheat the Air Fryer to 390°F for 3 minutes. Pat the lamb dry using a towel. Remove the fat and rub the meat with mustard. Blitz the rinds with herbs, Parmesan cheese, lemon zest and the seasonings. Season the joint. Place the meat in the Air Fryer and drizzle with oil. Roast the meat for around 15 minutes.

For the wedges, start by peeling and coring the pumpkin; then coat it with oil. Season the pumpkin and set aside. Remove lamb from the Air Fryer and put on a serving dish. Place the pumpkin wedges in the Air Fryer and roast for 18 minutes. Once ready, serve the meat with the salad and the wedges.

Sweet Homemade Beef Satay

Total Time: 25 min | **Serves**: 4 | **Per serving**: Cal 441; Net Carbs 6.5g; Fat 25.8g; Protein 53g

Ingredients

2 lb flank steaks, cut in long strips
2 tbsp fish sauce
2 tbsp soy sauce, sugar-free
2 tbsp swerve sweetener
2 tbsp garlic, ground

2 tbsp ginger, ground
2 tsp hot sauce
1 cup chopped cilantro, divided into two
½ cup roasted peanuts, chopped

Directions

Preheat the Air Fryer to 400°F.

In a zipper bag, add the beef, fish sauce, swerve sweetener, garlic, soy sauce, ginger, half of the cilantro, and hot sauce. Zip the bag and massage the ingredients with your hands to mix them well.

Open the bag, remove the beef, shake off the excess marinade and place the beef strips in the fryer basket in a single layer. Try to avoid overlapping.

Close the Air Fryer and cook for 5 minutes. Turn the beef and cook further for 5 minutes. Dish the cooked meat in a serving platter, garnish with the chopped peanuts and the remaining cilantro. Serve with a side of cauli rice and tomato sauce.

Easy Beef Meatloaf with herbs

Total Time: 30 min | **Serves**: 4 | **Per serving**: Cal 312; Net Carbs 5.2g; Fat 15g; Protein 34g

Ingredients

1 lb ground beef
2 eggs, lightly beaten
½ cup pork rinds, crushed
2 garlic cloves, crushed

1 onion, finely chopped
2 tbsp tomato puree, sugar-free
1 tsp mixed dried herbs

Directions

Line a loaf pan that fits in your fryer with baking paper.

In a bowl, mix beef, eggs, pork rinds, garlic, onion, puree, and herbs. Press the mixture into the pan and slide in the air fryer. Cook for 25 minutes at 380°F.

Turmeric Liver Curry

Total Time: 18 min | **Serves:** 2 | **Per serving:** Cal 212; Net Carbs 7.5g; Fat 7g; Protein 26g

Ingredients

½ lb beef liver
1 onion, sliced
1 large tomato, chopped
1 clove garlic, minced
1 tbsp ginger, grated
1 tbsp paprika
½ tbsp chili powder

1 tbsp cumin powder
½ tbsp ground coriander
½ tbsp turmeric
½ tbsp Garam Masala
4 drops liquid stevia
Cilantro leaves for garnish

Directions

In a skillet, fry the onion on medium heat until it tenders. Add the grated ginger and the garlic. Keep stirring. Add the powdered spices, then fry for 3 more minutes.

Meanwhile, season the liver with salt and pepper. Place the liver in the Air Fryer and cook it for 15 minutes at 350°F. Remove the liver from the Air Fryer and transfer it to the skillet. Add the tomato, stevia and a little bit of water until everything is cooked. Garnish with cilantro.

Ginger Ground Beef Kebab Skewers

Total Time: 25 min | **Serves:** 2 | **Per serving:** Cal 331; Net Carbs 2.5g; Fat 22g; Protein 33g

Ingredients

½ lb ground beef
½ large onion
1 medium green chili
½ tbsp chili powder

1 minced clove garlic
A pinch of ginger
1 tbsp Garam Masala
3 tbsp pork rinds, crushed

Directions

Grate 1 pinch of ginger and garlic. Chop and deseed the chili. Chop the onion. Mix ginger, garlic, chili and onion with ground beef. Add the powdered spices. Add a few pork rinds and salt.

Shape the beef into fat sausages around short wooden skewers. Set the skewers aside for 1 hour, then cook them in a preheated Air Fryer for 25 minutes at 350°F.

Cayenne-Coated Beef Steaks

Total Time: 15 min | **Serves:** 2 | **Per serving:** Cal 568; Net Carbs 1.7g; Fat 42g; Protein 47g

Ingredients

2 beef steaks, 1-inch thick
½ tsp black pepper
½ tsp cayenne pepper

1 tbsp olive oil
½ tsp hot paprika
Salt and black pepper to taste

Directions

Preheat the air fryer to 390°F, if needed.

Mix olive oil, black pepper, cayenne, paprika, salt and pepper and rub onto steaks.

Spread evenly. Put the steaks in the fryer, and cook for 6 minutes, turning them halfway through cooking

Jalapeño Baby Back Ribs

Total Time: 30 min | **Serves:** 4 | **Per serving:** Cal 631; Net Carbs 2.9g; Fat 67g; Protein 57g

Ingredients

1 slab baby back ribs
1 tbsp ginger, grated
1 scallion, minced
½ tbsp fresh cilantro, chopped
1 jalapeño pepper, seeded and chopped
1 clove garlic, minced
½ cup orange juice
2 tbsp sesame oil

Directions

Put the ingredients inside a plastic bag overnight. Reserve the marinade.

Place the ribs vertically in the Air Fryer. Cook for 30 minutes at 365°F.

Meanwhile, put the marinade in a deep cooking pan. Cook the marinade on medium heat for 5 minutes.

Brush the ribs with the marinade.

Thyme Lamb Chops with Parsnips

Total Time: 25 min | **Serves:** 2 | **Per serving:** Cal 527; Net Carbs 6.5g; Fat 41g; Protein 17g

Ingredients

2 lamb chops
2 tbsp olive oil
2 garlic cloves, crushed
Salt and black pepper to taste
A handful of fresh thyme, chopped
2 parsnips, cubed

Directions

Rub the chops with oil, garlic, salt and black pepper.

Put thyme in the fryer, and place the chops on top. Oil the parsnip chunks and sprinkle with salt and pepper.

Arrange the parsnips next to the chops, and cook on 360°F for 14 minutes, turning once halfway through cooking.

Prosciutto Wrapped Lamb Chops

Total Time: 20 min | **Serves:** 4 | **Per serving:** Cal 623; Net Carbs 3.2g; Fat 38g; Protein 63g

Ingredients

2 lb lamb rack, cut into quarters
2 balls fresh mozzarella cheese, sliced
4 leaves sage
4 slices thin prosciutto
2 tbsp olive oil

Directions

Preheat the Air Fryer to 350°F. Make a deep pocket in each of the lamb chops.

Stuff the pockets with mozzarella cheese. Put a sage leaf on the top of every chop.

Wrap each chop with a slice of prosciutto. Pour olive oil on the lamb and cook for 15 minutes.

PORK RECIPES

Stuffed Pork Loins in Bacon Wraps

Total Time: 45 min | **Serves**: 4 | **Per serving**: Cal 604; Net Carbs 2.8g; Fat 51.8g; Protein 30g

Ingredients

16 bacon slices
16 oz pork tenderloin
Salt and black pepper to season
1 cup spinach
3 oz cream cheese

1 small onion, sliced
1 tbsp olive oil
1 clove garlic, minced
½ tsp dried thyme
½ tsp dried rosemary

Directions

Place the tenderloin on a chopping board, cover it with a plastic wrap and pound it using a kitchen hammer to be 2-inches flat and square. Trim the uneven sides with a knife to have a perfect square. Set aside on a flat plate.

On the same chopping board, place and weave the bacon slices into a square of the size of the pork. Place the pork on the bacon weave and leave them aside for now.

Put a skillet over medium heat on a stove top, add the olive oil, onions, and garlic; sauté until transparent.

Add the spinach, ½ tsp rosemary, ½ tsp thyme, a bit of salt, and pepper. Stir with a spoon and allow the spinach to wilt.

Stir in the cream cheese, until the mixture is even. Turn the heat off.

Preheat the Air Fryer to 360°F.

Spoon and spread the spinach mixture onto the pork loin. Roll up the bacon and pork over the spinach stuffing. Secure the ends with toothpicks. Season with more salt and pepper.

Place in the fryer basket and cook it for 15 minutes. Flip to other side and cook for another 5 minutes.

Once ready, remove and place it on a clean chopping board. Let it sit for 4 minutes before slicing.

Serve with steamed green veggies.

Cheddar Pulled Pork with Bacon

Total Time: 50 min | **Serves**: 2 | **Per serving**: Cal 765; Net Carbs 6.3g; Fat 68g; Protein 34g

Ingredients

½ pound pork steak
1 tsp steak seasoning
Salt and black pepper to taste
5 thick bacon slices, chopped

1 cup grated cheddar cheese
½ tbsp Worcestershire sauce
2 hamburger buns, zero carbs, halved

Directions

Preheat the Air Fryer to 400°F.

Place the pork steak in a plate and season with pepper, salt, and the steak seasoning. Pat it with your hands. Slide out the fryer basket and place the pork in it. Grill it for 15 minutes, turn it using tongs, slide the fryer in and continue cooking for 6 minutes.

Once ready, remove the steak onto a chopping board and use two forks to shred the pork into small pieces.

Place the chopped bacon in a small heatproof bowl and place the bowl in the fryer basket. Close the Air Fryer and cook the bacon at 370°F for 10 minutes.

Remove the bacon into a bigger heatproof bowl, add the pulled pork, Worcestershire sauce, and the cheddar cheese. Season with salt and pepper as desired.

Place the bowl in the fryer basket and cook at 350°For 4 minutes. Slide out the fryer basket, stir the mixture with a spoon, slide the fryer basket back in and cook further for 1 minute. Spoon to scoop the meat into the halved buns and serve with a cheese or tomato dip.

BBQ Pork Ribs

Total Time: 5 hrs 35 min | **Serves**: 3 | **Per serving**: Cal 376; Net Carbs 3.3g; Fat 29.3g; Protein 21.7g

Ingredients

1 lb pork ribs
1 tsp soy sauce, sugar-free
Salt and black pepper to taste
1 tsp oregano
1 tbsp + 1 tbsp erythritol

3 tbsp reduced sugar barbecue sauce
2 cloves garlic, minced
1 tbsp cayenne pepper
1 tsp sesame oil

Directions

Put the chops on a chopping board and use a knife to cut them into smaller pieces of desired sizes.

Put them in a mixing bowl, add the soy sauce, salt, pepper, oregano, one tablespoon of erythritol, barbecue sauce, garlic, cayenne pepper, and sesame oil.

Mix well and place the pork in the fridge to marinate in the spices for 5 hours.

Preheat the Air Fryer to 350°F. Open the Air Fryer and place the ribs in the fryer basket. Slide the fryer basket in and cook for 15 minutes.

Open the Air fryer, turn the ribs using tongs, apply the remaining erythritol on it with a brush, close the Air Fryer, and continue cooking for 10 minutes.

Paprika Pork Chops

Total Time: 25 min | **Serves**: 3 | **Per serving**: Cal 376; Net Carbs 2.6g; Fat 16.9g; Protein 33.9g

Ingredients

3 lean pork chops
Salt and black pepper to taste
2 eggs, cracked into a bowl
1 tbsp water
1 cup pork rinds, crushed
½ tsp garlic powder

3 tsp paprika
1 ½ tsp oregano
½ tsp cayenne pepper
¼ tsp dry mustard
1 lemon, zested

Directions

Put the pork chops on a chopping board and use a knife to trim off any excess fat. Add the water to the eggs and whisk it. Set aside.

In another bowl, add the pork rinds, salt, pepper, garlic powder, paprika, oregano, cayenne pepper, lemon zest, and dry mustard. Use a fork to mix evenly.

Preheat the Air Fryer to 380°F and after grease the fryer basket with cooking spray.

In the egg mixture, dip each pork chop and then in the pork rind mixture.

Place the breaded chops in the fryer basket. Don't spray with cooking spray. The fat in the chops will be enough oil to cook them. Close the Air Fryer and cook for 10 minutes. Flip to other side and cook for another 5 minutes.

Once ready, place the chops on a chopping board to rest for 3 minutes before slicing.

Bacon Rolls with Sausage Sticks

Total Time: 2 hrs | **Serves**: 8 | **Per serving**: Cal 455; Net Carbs 8.3g; Fat 39.6g; Protein 18.7g

Ingredients

Sausage:

8 bacon strips
8 pork sausages

8 medium length bamboo skewers

Relish:

8 large tomatoes
1 clove garlic, peeled
1 small onion, peeled
3 tbsp chopped parsley

Salt and black pepper to taste
2 tbsp swerve sugar
1 tsp smoked paprika
1 tbsp vinegar

Directions

Start with the relish; add the tomatoes, garlic, and onion in a food processor. Blitz them for 10 seconds until the mixture is pulpy.

Pour the pulp into a saucepan, add the vinegar, salt, pepper, and place it over medium heat. Bring it to simmer for 10 minutes.

Add the paprika and sugar. Stir with a spoon and simmer for 10 minutes until pulpy and thick. Turn off the heat, transfer the relish to a bowl and chill it for an hour. In 30 minutes after putting the relish in the refrigerator, move on to the sausages.

Wrap each sausage with a bacon strip neatly and stick in a bamboo skewer at the end of the sausage to secure the bacon ends.

Open the Air Fryer, place 4 wrapped sausages in the fryer basket and cook for 12 minutes at 350°F. Repeat the cooking process for the remaining wrapped sausages. Remove the relish from the refrigerator. Serve the sausages and relish with turnip mash.

Soy & Cinnamon Marinated Pork Tenderloins

Total Time: 60 min | **Serves:** 4 | **Per serving:** Cal 522; Net Carbs 1.6g; Fat 18g; Protein 74g

Ingredients

4 pork tenderloins
1 cinnamon quill
1 tbsp olive oil

1 tbsp soy sauce, sugar-free
Salt and black pepper to taste

Directions

In a bowl, add pork, cinnamon, olive oil, soy sauce, salt and black pepper into. Stir to coat well.

Let sit at room temperature for 25-35 minutes. Put the pork into the air fryer, and a little bit of marinade. Cook at 380°F for 14 minutes, turning once halfway through cooking. Serve hot!

Basil Pork Burgers

Total Time: 35 min | **Serves**: 2 | **Per serving**: Cal 470; Net Carbs 6g; Fat 42g; Protein 22g

Ingredients

½ lb minced pork
1 medium onion, chopped
1 tbsp mixed herbs
2 tsp garlic powder
1 tsp dried basil

1 tbsp tomato puree
1 tsp mustard
Salt and black pepper to taste
2 zero carbs bread Buns, halved

Assembling:

1 large onion, sliced in 2-inch rings
1 large tomato, sliced in 2-inch rings

2 small lettuce leaves, cleaned
4 slices cheddar cheese

Directions

In a bowl, add the minced pork, chopped onion, mixed herbs, garlic powder, dried basil, tomato puree, mustard, salt, and pepper. Use your hands to mix them evenly.

Form two patties out of the mixture and place them on a flat plate.

Preheat the Air Fryer to 370°F. Place the pork patties in the fryer basket, close the Air Fryer, and cook them for 15 minutes.

Slide out the fryer basket and turn the patties. Reduce the temperature to 350°F and continue cooking for 5 minutes. Once ready, remove them onto a plate and start assembling the burger.

Place two halves of the bun on a clean flat surface. Add the lettuce in both, then a patty each, followed by an onion ring each, a tomato ring each, and then 2 slices of cheddar cheese each. Cover the buns with their other halves.

Serve with a side of sugar-free ketchup and some turnip fries.

Herby Pork Roast

Total Time: 4 hrs 40 min | **Serves**: 4 | **Per serving**: Cal 587; Net Carbs 1g; Fat 54.2g; Protein 22g

Ingredients

1 ½ lb pork belly
1 ½ tsp garlic powder
1 ½ tsp coriander powder
Salt and black pepper to taste
1 ½ dried thyme

1 ½ tsp dried oregano
1 ½ tsp cumin powder
3 cups water
1 lemon, halved

Directions

Leave the pork to air dry for about 3 hours.

In a small bowl, add garlic powder, coriander powder, salt, black pepper, thyme, oregano, and cumin powder. After the pork is well dried, poke holes all around it using a fork.

Smear the oregano rub thoroughly on all sides with your hands and squeeze the lemon juice all over it. Leave to sit for 5 minutes, while you preheat the Air Fryer to 340 F. Put the pork in the center of the fryer basket, close the Air Fryer and cook for 30 minutes.

Turn the pork with the help of two spatulas, increase the temperature to 350°F and continue cooking for 25 minutes. Once ready, remove it and place it in on a chopping board to sit for 4 minutes before slicing. Serve the pork slices with a side of sautéed asparagus and hot sauce.

Chili Tri-Color Pork Kebabs

Total Time: 90 min | **Serves**: 4 | **Per serving**: Cal 247; Net Carbs 2.5g; Fat 14.9g; Protein 28g

Ingredients

1 lb pork chops, cut in cubes
¼ cup soy sauce, sugar-free
2 tsp smoked paprika
1 tsp powdered chili

1 tsp garlic salt
1 tsp red chili flakes
1 tbsp vinegar
3 tbsp hot sauce

Skewing:

1 green pepper, cut in cubes
1 red pepper, cut in cubes
1 yellow squash, seeded and cubed

1 green squash, seeded in cubed
Salt and black pepper to taste

Directions

In a mixing bowl, add the pork cubes, soy sauce, smoked paprika, powdered chili, garlic salt, red chili flakes, white wine vinegar, and hot sauce. Mix them using a spoon.

Refrigerate to marinate them for 1 hour.

After an hour, remove the marinated pork from the fridge and preheat the Air Fryer to 370°F.

On each skewer, stick the pork cubes and vegetables in the order that you prefer.

Once the pork cubes and vegetables are finished, arrange the skewers in the fryer basket and grill them for 8 minutes. You can do them in batches.

Once ready, remove them onto the serving platter and serve with salad.

Rosemary Pork Rack with Nuts

Total Time: 53 min | **Serves**: 3 | **Per serving**: Cal 319; Net Carbs 1g; Fat 18g; Protein 27g

Ingredients

1 lb rack of pork
2 tbsp olive oil
1 clove garlic, minced
Salt and black pepper to taste

1 cup unsalted macadamia nuts, chopped
1 tbsp pork rinds, crushed
1 egg, beaten in a bowl
1 tbsp fresh rosemary, chopped

Directions

Add the olive oil and garlic to a bowl. Mix vigorously with a spoon to make garlic oil. Place the rack of pork on a chopping board and brush it with the garlic oil using a brush. Sprinkle with salt and pepper.

Preheat the Air Fryer to 320°F.

In a bowl, add the pork rinds, nuts, and rosemary. Mix with a spoon and set aside.

Brush the meat with the egg on all sides and sprinkle the nut mixture generously over the pork. Press with your hands to avoid the nut mixture from falling off. Put the coated pork in the fryer basket, close the Air Fryer, and roast for 30 minutes.

Then, increase the temperature to 390°F and cook further for 5 minutes. Once ready, remove the meat onto a chopping board. Allow sitting for 10 minutes before slicing it.

Serve with a side of parsnip fries and tomato dip.

Herby Mushroom Filled Pork Chops

Total Time: 40 min | **Serves:** 3 | **Per serving:** Cal 412; Net Carbs 1.2g; Fat 28g; Protein 28g

Ingredients

3 thick pork chops
A pinch of herbs
7 mushrooms, chopped

1 tbsp almond flour
1 tbsp lemon juice
Salt and black pepper, to taste

Directions

Preheat the Air Fryer to 350°F. Season each side of the meat with the salt and pepper. Arrange the chops in the Air Fryer and cook for 15 minutes at 350°F.

Meanwhile, cook the mushroom for 3 minutes, in a skillet, and stir in the lemon juice. Add the flour and then mix the herbs. Cook the mixture for 4 minutes. Then set aside.

Cut five pieces of foil for each of the chops. On every piece of foil put a chop in the middle and cover with the mushroom mixture. Fold the foil and seal around the chop. Cook the chops in the Air Fryer for 30 minutes.

Aromatic Pork Chops

Total Time: 140 min | **Serves**: 3 | **Per serving**: Cal 373; Net Carbs 3.1g; Fat 21.3g; Protein 24.2g

Ingredients

3 slices pork chops
2 garlic cloves, minced
4 stalks lemongrass, trimmed, chopped
2 shallots, chopped

2 tbsp olive oil
1 ¼ tsp soy sauce, sugar-free
1 ¼ tsp fish sauce
1 ½ tsp black pepper

Directions

In a bowl, add the garlic, lemongrass, shallots, olive oil, soy sauce, fish sauce, and black pepper; mix well.

Add the pork chops, coat them with the mixture and allow to marinate for around 2 hours to get nice and savory. Preheat the Air Fryer to 400°F.

Cooking in 2 to 3 batches, remove and shake each pork chop from the marinade and place it in the fryer basket. Cook it for 7 minutes. Turn the pork chops and cook further for 5 minutes. Remove the chops and serve with sautéed asparagus.

Mustard-Sweet Pork Balls

Total Time: 25 min | **Serves**: 6 | **Per serving**: Cal 225; Net Carbs 1g; Fat 17g; Protein 13g

Ingredients

1 lb ground pork
1 large onion, chopped
½ tsp erythritol
2 tsp mustard

½ cup chopped basil leaves
Salt and black pepper to taste
2 tbsp cheddar cheese, grated

Directions

In a mixing bowl, add the ground pork, onion, erythritol, mustard, basil leaves, salt, pepper, and cheddar cheese. Mix everything well.

Use your hands to form bite-size balls. Place them in the fryer basket and cook them at 400°F for 10 minutes. Slide out the fryer basket and shake it to toss the meatballs.

Cook for 5 minutes. Remove to a wire rack and serve with marinara sauce.

Simple Shirred Eggs

Total Time: 20 min | **Serves**: 2 | **Per serving**: Cal 279; Net Carbs 1.8g; Fat 20g; Protein 21g

Ingredients

2 tsp butter, for greasing
4 eggs, divided
2 tbsp heavy cream
4 slices pork ham

3 tbsp Parmesan cheese, shredded
¼ tsp paprika
Salt and black pepper to taste
2 tsp chives, chopped

Directions

Preheat the air fryer to 320°F.

Grease a pie pan with the butter. Arrange the ham slices on the bottom of the pan to cover it completely.

Whisk one egg along with the heavy cream, salt and pepper, in a small bowl. Pour the mixture over the ham slices.

Crack the other eggs over the ham. Sprinkle the Parmesan cheese and cook for 14 minutes. Sprinkle with paprika and garnish with chives.

Sweet Pork Chops

Total Time: 17 min | **Serves:** 3 | **Per serving:** Cal 351; Net Carbs 2g; Fat 19.5g; Protein 41.5g

Ingredients

3 pork chops, ½-inch thick
Salt and black pepper to taste

1 tbsp erythritol
3 tbsp mustard

Directions

In a bowl, add erythritol, mustard, salt, and pepper and mix well. Add the pork and toss to coat. Place in the fryer basket and cook at 350°F for 6 minutes. Flip and cook for 6 minutes.

Almond Crusted Pork Chops

Total Time: 25 min | **Serves:** 4 | **Per serving:** Cal 345; Net Carbs 1.2g; Fat 21g; Protein 42g

Ingredients

4 pork chops, center-cut
2 tbsp almond flour
2 tbsp sour cream

Salt and black pepper to taste
½ cup pork rinds, crushed

Directions

Coat the chops with almond flour. Drizzle the cream over the chops. Spread the pork rinds into a bowl, and coat each pork chop with them. Spray with oil and arrange them into the air fryer. Cook for 14 minutes at 380°F, turning once halfway through cooking.

Cinnamon Pork Patties

Total Time: 25 min | **Serves:** 2 | **Per serving:** Cal 505; Net Carbs 2.5g; Fat 21g; Protein 64g

Ingredients

12 oz ground pork
1 cup pork rinds, crushed
2 eggs, beaten

½ tsp ground cumin
½ tsp ground cinnamon
Salt and black pepper to taste

Directions

In a bowl, add all the ingredients. Mix with hands. Shape into patties. Arrange the patties inside the Air Fryer and cook for 14 minutes at 340°F, turning once halfway through cooking.

CHICKEN AND TURKEY RECIPES

Sweet Chili Chicken Breasts

Total Time: 55 min | **Serves**: 3 | **Per serving**: Cal 226; Net Carbs 2g; Fat 8g; Protein 18.2g

Ingredients

2 chicken breasts, cubed
Salt and black pepper to taste
1 cup almond flour
3 eggs
½ cup Apple Cider vinegar
½ tsp ginger paste
½ tsp garlic paste

1 tbsp swerve sweetener
2 red chilies, minced
2 tbsp tomato puree
1 red pepper
1 green pepper
1 tsp paprika
4 tbsp water

Directions

Preheat the Air Fryer to 350°F. Pour the almond flour in a bowl, crack the eggs into it, add the salt and pepper. Whisk it using a fork or whisk.

Put the chicken in the flour mixture. Mix to coat the chicken with it using a wooden spatula. Place the chicken in the fryer basket, spray them with cooking spray, and fry them for 8 minutes.

Pull out the fryer basket, shake it to toss the chicken, and spray again with cooking spray. Keeping cooking for 7 minutes or until golden and crispy.

Remove the chicken into a plate and set aside.

Put the red, yellow, and green peppers on a chopping board. Using a knife, cut them open and deseed them. Cut the flesh in long strips.

In a bowl, add the water, apple cider vinegar, swerve sweetener, ginger and garlic puree, red chili, tomato puree, and smoked paprika. Mix with a fork.

Place a skillet over medium heat on a stove top and spray it with cooking spray.

Add the chicken to it and the pepper strips. Stir and cook until the peppers are sweaty but still crunchy. Pour the chili mixture on the chicken, stir, and bring it to simmer for 10 minutes. Turn off the heat.

Dish the chicken chili sauce into a serving bowl and serve with a side of steamed cauli rice.

Homemade Jerk Chicken Wings

Total Time: 16 hrs 42 min | **Serves**: 4 | **Per serving**: Cal 351; Net Carbs 4.2g; Fat 13.8g; Protein 50.7g

Ingredients

2 lb chicken wings
1 tbsp olive oil
3 cloves garlic, minced
1 tsp chili powder
½ tsp cinnamon powder
½ tsp allspice
1 habanero pepper, seeded
1 tbsp soy sauce, sugar-free

½ tsp white pepper
¼ cup red wine vinegar
3 tbsp lime juice
2 scallions, chopped
½ tbsp grated ginger
½ tbsp chopped fresh thyme
⅓ tbsp erythritol
½ tsp salt

Directions

In a large bowl, add the olive oil, soy sauce, garlic, habanero pepper, allspice, cinnamon powder, cayenne pepper, white pepper, salt, erythritol, thyme, ginger, scallions, lime juice, and red wine vinegar. Use a spoon to mix them well.

Add the chicken wings to the marinade mixture and coat it well with the mixture.

Cover the bowl with cling film and refrigerate the chicken to marinate it for 16 hours.

Preheat the Air Fryer to 400°F. Remove the chicken from the fridge, drain all the liquid, and pat each wing dry using a paper towel.

Place half of the wings in the fryer basket and cook it for 16 minutes. Shake the fryer basket to toss the chicken halfway through. Remove onto a serving platter and repeat the cooking process for the remaining chicken. Serve the jerk wings with a blue cheese dip or ranch dressing.

Herby Chicken Thighs with Tomatoes

Total Time: 20 min | **Serves**: 2 | **Per serving**: Cal 285; Net Carbs 2.1g; Fat 15g; Protein 21g

Ingredients

2 chicken thighs
1 cup tomatoes, quartered
4 cloves garlic, minced
½ tsp dried tarragon

½ tsp olive oil
¼ tsp red pepper flakes
Salt and black pepper to taste

Directions

Preheat the Air Fryer to 390°F.

Add the tomatoes, red pepper flakes, tarragon, garlic, and olive oil to a medium bowl. Mix it well. In a large ramekin, add the chicken and top it with the tomato mixture.

Place the ramekin in the fryer basket and roast for 10 minutes.

After baking, carefully remove the ramekin.

Plate the chicken thighs, spoon the cooking juice over and serve with a side of cauli rice.

Amazing Chicken Lollipop

Total Time: 20 min | **Serves**: 3 | **Per serving**: Cal 276; Net Carbs 2g; Fat 10.4g; Protein 14.9g

Ingredients

1 lb mini chicken drumsticks
½ tsp soy sauce, sugar-free
1 tsp lime juice
Salt and black pepper to taste
1 tsp arrowroot starch
½ tsp minced garlic
½ tsp chili powder
½ tsp chopped coriander

½ tsp garlic ginger paste
1 tsp vinegar
1 tsp chili paste
½ tsp egg, beaten
1 tsp paprika
1 tsp almond flour
2 tsp erythritol

Directions

Mix the garlic-ginger paste, chili powder, erythritol, paprika powder, chopped coriander, plain vinegar, egg, garlic, and salt in a bowl.

Add the chicken drumsticks and toss to coat thoroughly. Stir in the arrowroot starch, almond flour, and lime juice.

Preheat the Air Fryer to 350°F.

Remove each drumstick, shake off the excess marinade, and place in a single layer in the fryer basket. Cook them for 5 minutes.

Slide out the fryer basket, spray the chicken with cooking spray and continue cooking for 5 minutes.

Remove to a serving platter and serve with a tomato dip.

Sweet Chicken Kabobs with Salsa Verde

Total Time: 35 min | **Serves**: 3 | **Per serving**: Cal 468; Net Carbs 6.1g; Fat 29g; Protein 43g

Ingredients

3 chicken breasts
Salt to taste
1 tbsp chili powder
¼ cup erythritol
½ cup soy sauce, sugar-free

2 red peppers
1 green pepper
7 mushrooms
2 tbsp sesame seeds

Salsa verde:

1 garlic clove
2 tbsp olive oil
Zest and juice from 1 lime

A pinch of salt
¼ cup fresh parsley, chopped

Directions

Put the chicken breasts on a clean flat surface and cut them in 2-inch cubes with a knife. Add them to a bowl, along with the chili powder, salt, erythritol, soy sauce, sesame seeds, and spray them with cooking spray. Toss to coat and set aside. Place the peppers on the chopping board. Use a knife to open, deseed and cut in cubes. Likewise, slice the mushrooms in halves.

Start sticking up the ingredients: stick 1 red pepper, then green, a chicken cube, and a mushroom half. Repeat the sticking arrangement until the skewer is full. Repeat the process until all the ingredients are finished.

Preheat the Air Fryer to 330°F. Brush the kabobs with soy sauce mixture and place into the basket. Grease with cooking spray and grill for 20 minutes. Flip halfway through.

Blend all salsa verde ingredients in a food processor until obtaining a chunky paste. Remove the kabobs when ready and serve with a side of salsa verde.

Chicken Tenders with Tarragon

Total Time: 17 min | **Serves**: 2 | **Per serving**: Cal 230; Net Carbs 2g; Fat 12.5g; Protein 18g

Ingredients

2 chicken tenders
Salt and black pepper to taste

½ cup dried tarragon
1 tsp unsalted butter

Directions

Preheat the Air Fryer to 390°F.

Lay out a 12 X 12 inch cut of foil on a flat surface.

Place the chicken breasts on the foil, sprinkle the tarragon on both, and share the butter onto both breasts. Sprinkle salt and pepper on them. Loosely wrap the foil around the breasts to enable air flow. Place the wrapped chicken in the fryer basket and cook for 12 minutes.

Remove the chicken and carefully unwrap the foil. Serve the chicken with the sauce extract and steamed mixed veggies.

Asian-Style Marinated Chicken

Total Time: 20 min | **Serves**: 6 | **Per serving:** Cal 523; Net Carbs 2.5g; Fat 46g; Protein 31g

Ingredients

2 lbs chicken breasts, cut into cubes
¼ cup pork rinds, crushed
2 large eggs
6 tbsp almond flour
1 tbsp baking powder
½ cup vegetable oil
4 tbsp sesame oil

2 tbsp fresh ginger root, grated
½ cup green onion, chopped
½ cup water
¼ cup white vinegar
1 ½ tbsp liquid stevia
2 tbsp soy sauce
¼ cup oyster sauce

Directions

Preheat the Air Fryer to 390°F. Coat the chicken cubes with the pork rinds, then set aside.

In a large bowl, beat eggs, salt, and pepper until the mixture is smooth. Add flour and baking powder, and beat until there are no lumps.

Coat the chicken and place it on the rack of the Air Fryer. Pour 2 tablespoons of oil and cook it for 15 minutes. Remove and set aside.

In a skillet, heat oil. Then stir in sesame oil, onion, and ginger. Cook and keep stirring for 2-3 minutes.

Add the water, the vinegar, the stevia and boil the mixture. In soy sauce, dissolve pork rinds, and add vinegar and oyster sauce.

Keep stirring until the sauce thickens. Add the chicken and let simmer for 10-15 minutes.

Saturday Garlic Chicken Stuffed

Total Time: 55 min | **Serves**: 3 | **Per serving**: Cal 343; Net Carbs 2.5g; Fat 15.8g; Protein 35g

Ingredients

1 (3 lb) small chicken
1 ½ tbsp olive oil
Salt and black pepper to taste
1 cup pork rinds, crushed
⅓ cup chopped sage

⅓ cup chopped thyme
2 cloves garlic, crushed
1 brown onion, chopped
3 tbsp butter
2 eggs, beaten

Directions

Rinse the chicken gently, pat dry with a paper towel and remove any excess fat with a knife. Place it aside. On a stove top, place a pan. Add the butter, garlic, and onion and sauté to brown.

Add the eggs, sage, thyme, pepper, and salt. Mix well. Cook for 20 seconds and turn the heat off.

Stuff the chicken with the mixture into the cavity. Then, tie the legs of the spatchcock with a butcher's twine and brush with the olive oil. Rub the top and sides of the chicken generously with salt and pepper.

Preheat the Air Fryer to 390°F. Place the spatchcock into the fryer basket and roast it for 25 minutes. Turn the chicken over and continue cooking for a further 10-15 minutes but you can check it throughout the cooking time to ensure it doesn't dry or overcooks.

Remove to a chopping board and wrap it with aluminum foil. Let it rest for 10 minutes.

Rosemary Chicken with Egg Noodles

Total Time: 30 min | **Serves**: 4 | **Per serving**: Cal 523; Net Carbs 1.8g; Fat 34g; Protein 41g

Ingredients

4 chicken breasts, skinless and boneless
Salt and black pepper to taste
1 tbsp rosemary
<u>Noodles:</u>
2 cups almond flour
½ tbsp salt

1 tbsp tomato paste
1 tbsp red pepper
1 tbsp all spices

2 eggs, beaten

Directions

Preheat the Air Fryer to 350°F. Coat the chicken with 1 tbsp of butter, salt, and pepper. Arrange the chicken breasts in the basket and cook for 20 minutes.

For the noodles, combine flour, salt, and egg, and make a dough. Place the dough on a floured surface. Knead and cover it. Set aside for 30 minutes.

Roll the dough on a floured surface. When the batter thins, cut into thin strips and let dry for 1 hour.

Meanwhile, take the chicken out of the Air Fryer and put it aside. Boil the chicken broth and add noodles, tomato paste, and red pepper. Cook for 5 minutes.

Add the spices and stir in the noodles. Salt and pepper to taste.

Serve the noodles with the air fried chicken.

Prosciutto & Brie Chicken Breasts

Total Time: 25 min | **Serves**: 2 | **Per serving**: Cal 262; Net Carbs 3g; Fat 16g; Protein 24g

Ingredients

2 chicken breasts
1 tbsp olive oil
Salt and black pepper to taste

1 cup semi-dried tomatoes, sliced
½ cup brie cheese, halved
4 slices thin prosciutto

Directions

Preheat the Air Fryer to 365°F.

Put the chicken on a chopping board. With a knife, cut a small incision deep enough to make stuffing on both. Insert one slice of cheese and 4 to 5 tomato slices into each chicken.

Lay the prosciutto on the chopping board. Put the chicken on one side of it and roll the prosciutto over the chicken making sure that both ends of the prosciutto meet under the chicken.

Drizzle the olive oil and sprinkle it with salt and pepper.

Put the chicken in the fryer basket. Cook it for 10 minutes. Turn the breasts over and cook for another 5 minutes.

Slice each chicken breast in half and serve with green tomato salad.

Chicken Drumsticks with Blue Cheese Sauce

Total Time: 2 hrs 30 min | **Serves**: 4 | **Per serving**: Cal 281; Net Carbs 2g; Fat 14.2g; Protein 14.8g

Ingredients

Drumsticks:

1 lb mini chicken drumsticks

3 tbsp butter

3 tbsp paprika

2 tsp powdered cumin

¼ cup hot sauce

1 tbsp erythritol

2 tbsp onion powder

2 tbsp garlic powder

Blue cheese sauce:

½ cup mayonnaise

1 cup blue cheese, crumbled

1 cup sour cream

1 ½ tsp garlic powder

1 ½ tsp onion powder

Salt and black pepper to taste

1 ½ tsp cayenne pepper

1 ½ tsp white wine vinegar

2 tbsp buttermilk

1 ½ Worcestershire sauce, sugar-free

Directions

Start with the drumstick sauce; place a pan over medium heat on a stove top.

Add the butter, once melted add the hot sauce, paprika, garlic, onion, erythritol, and cumin; mix well. Cook the mixture for 5 minutes or until the sauce reduces. Turn off the heat and let it cool.

Put the drumsticks in a bowl, pour half of the sauce on it, and mix. Save the remaining sauce for serving. Refrigerate the drumsticks to marinate them for 2 hours.

Make the blue cheese sauce: in a jug, add the sour cream, blue cheese, mayonnaise, garlic powder, onion powder, buttermilk, cayenne pepper, vinegar, Worcestershire sauce, pepper, and salt.

Using a stick blender, blend the ingredients until they are well mixed with no large lumps. Adjust the salt and pepper taste as desired.

Preheat the Air Fryer to 350°F.

Remove the drumsticks from the fridge and place them in the fryer basket.

Cook for 15 minutes. Turn the drumsticks with tongs every 5 minutes to ensure that they are evenly cooked. Remove the drumsticks into a serving bowl and pour the remaining sauce over it.

Serve the drumsticks with the blue cheese sauce and a side of celery sticks.

Turmeric Chicken Breasts

Total Time: 22 min | **Serves**: 3 | **Per serving**: Cal 164; Net Carbs 2g; Fat 6.8g; Protein 24.8g

Ingredients

3 chicken breasts
Salt to taste

¼ cup chili sauce, reduced sugar
3 tbsp turmeric

Directions

Preheat the Air Fryer to 390°F. In a bowl, add the salt, sweet chili sauce, and turmeric. Mix evenly with a spoon. Place the chicken breasts on a clean flat surface and with a brush, apply the turmeric sauce lightly on the chicken.

Place them in the fryer basket and grill for 18 minutes. Turn them halfway through. Remove them and serve with a side of steamed mixed greens.

Paprika Roasted Whole Chicken

Total Time: 50 min | **Serves**: 2 | **Per serving**: Cal 317; Net Carbs 3g; Fat 21.4g; Protein 18.9g

Ingredients

1 (3 lb) whole chicken, on the bone
Salt and black pepper to taste
1 tsp chili powder
1 tsp garlic powder
4 tsp oregano

2 tsp coriander powder
2 tsp cumin powder
2 tbsp olive oil
4 tsp paprika
1 lime, juiced

Directions

In a bowl, pour the oregano, garlic powder, chili powder, ground coriander, paprika, cumin powder, pepper, salt, and olive oil. Mix well to create a rub for the chicken.

Add the chicken and with gloves on your hands rub the spice mixture well on the chicken. Refrigerate the chicken to marinate it for 20 minutes.

Preheat the Air Fryer to 350°F. Remove the chicken from the refrigerator; place in the fryer basket and cook for 20 minutes.

Use a skewer to poke the chicken to ensure that it is clear of juices. If not, cook the chicken further for 5 to 10 minutes. Allow the chicken to sit for 10 minutes. After, drizzle the lime juice over it. Serve with a green salad.

Curried Chicken Breasts

Total Time: 98 min | **Serves**: 2 | **Per serving**: Cal 428; Net Carbs 6.8g; Fat 23.5g; Protein 42g

Ingredients

2 chicken breasts
1 tbsp mayonnaise
2 eggs
1 tsp chili pepper

1 tsp curry powder
1 tbsp swerve sweetener
1 tsp soy sauce, sugar-free

Directions

Put the chicken cutlets on a clean flat surface and use a knife to slice in diagonal pieces. Gently pound them to become thinner using a rolling pin.

Place them in a bowl and add soy sauce, swerve sweetener, curry powder, and chili pepper. Mix well and leave to marinate in the fridge for around an hour.

Preheat the Air Fryer to 350°F.

Remove the chicken and crack the eggs into it. Add the mayonnaise and mix.

Remove each chicken piece and shake it well to remove as much liquid from it. Place them in the fryer basket, close the Air Fryer, and cook for 8 minutes. Turn and cook further for 6 minutes.

Remove them onto a serving platter and continue the cooking process for the remaining pieces of chicken. Serve the curried chicken with a side of steam greens.

Power Green Hot Drumsticks

Total Time: 25 min | **Serves**: 4 | **Per serving:** Cal 275; Net Carbs 1.9g; Fat 17.5g; Protein 26g

Ingredients

4 chicken drumsticks, boneless, skinless
2 tbsp green curry paste
3 tbsp coconut cream

Salt and black pepper to taste
½ fresh jalapeno chili, finely chopped
A handful of fresh parsley, roughly chopped

Directions

In a bowl, add the drumsticks, paste, cream, salt, black pepper and jalapeno, and coat the chicken. Arrange the drumsticks into the air fryer and cook for 6 minutes at 400°F, flipping once halfway through cooking. Serve with the fresh cilantro.

Broccoli Chicken Cheesy Casserole

Total Time: 53 min | **Serves**: 3 | **Per serving**: Cal 321; Net Carbs 2g; Fat 13.4g; Protein 35g

Ingredients

3 chicken breasts
Salt and black pepper to taste
1 cup shredded cheddar cheese

1 broccoli head
½ cup mushroom soup cream
½ cup low carbs croutons

Directions

Preheat the Air Fryer to 390°F.

Place the chicken breasts on a clean flat surface and season with salt and pepper. Grease with cooking spray and place them in the fryer basket. Close the Air Fryer and cook for 13 minutes.

Meanwhile, place the broccoli on the chopping board and use a knife to chop. Remove them onto the chopping board, let cool, and cut into bite-size pieces.

In a bowl, add the chicken, broccoli, cheddar cheese, and mushroom soup cream and mix well.

Scoop the mixture into a 3 X 3cm casserole dish, add the low carb croutons on top and spray with cooking spray. Put the dish in the fryer basket and cook for 10 minutes.

Tasty Barbecued Satay

Total Time: 15 min | **Serves**: 3 | **Per serving**: Cal 434; Net Carbs 6.8g; Fat 31g; Protein 29g

Ingredients

12 oz chicken tenders, boneless and skinless
½ cup soy sauce
¼ cup sesame oil
4 cloves garlic, chopped

4 scallions, chopped
1 tbsp fresh ginger, grated
2 tbsp sesame seeds, toasted
A pinch of black pepper

Directions

Start by skewering each tender and trim any excess fat.

Mix the rest of the ingredients in one large bowl. Add the skewered chicken and place them in the fridge for a period of 4 to 24 hours. Preheat the Air Fryer to 390°F. Pat the chicken until it is completely dry using a paper towel. Cook for 7-10 minutes.

Chicken with Cilantro Adobo

Total Time: 15 min | **Serves:** 2 | **Per serving:** Cal 419; Net Carbs 5.1g; Fat 19g; Protein 34g

Ingredients

2 chicken breasts, boneless and skinless
2 tbsp lime juice
1 tbsp fresh cilantro, minced
1 tbsp olive oil
3 garlic cloves, minced

1 green onion, minced
¼ tbsp ground cumin
¼ tbsp fresh thyme, minced
¼ tbsp fresh oregano, minced
Salt and black pepper to taste

Directions

Mix the ingredients in a resealable plastic bag and seal the bag.

Refrigerate for at least 3 hours. Then drain the marinade.

Using long tongs, moist paper toweling with the oil and coat the Air Fryer's rack. Set the heat to 340°F and time to 20 minutes. Don't forget to flip the chicken at least once in the cooking process.

Oregano Chicken Marsala

Total Time: 30 min | **Serves:** 4 | **Per serving:** Cal 488; Net Carbs 3.2g; Fat 43g; Protein 37g

Ingredients

¼ cup almond flour
½ tbsp dried oregano
4 chicken breasts, skinless and boneless
4 tbsp butter
4 tbsp olive oil

1 cup mushrooms, sliced
½ cup Marsala wine
Salt and black pepper to taste
¼ cup cooking sherry

Directions

Preheat the Air Fryer to 350°F.

In a bowl, combine the flour, the salt, the pepper, and the oregano. Coat the chicken with flour and arrange it on the rack of the Air Fryer. Pour over one tablespoon of oil and cook for 12 minutes.

After that, add the mushrooms and cook for 5 more minutes. Transfer the ingredients to a pan and pour wine and sherry. Let simmer for 10 minutes.

Chicken Breasts Wrapped in Bacon

Total Time: 21 min | **Serves**: 4 | **Per serving**: Cal 408; Net Carbs 1.5g; Fat 28g; Protein 27g

Ingredients

2 chicken breasts
8 oz onion and chive cream cheese
1 tbsp butter
6 turkey bacon

Salt to taste
1 tbsp fresh parsley, finely chopped
Juice from ½ lemon

Directions

Preheat the Air Fryer to 390°F.

Stretch out the bacon slightly and lay them on in 2 sets, that is 3 bacon strips together on each side.

Place the chicken breast on each bacon set and use a knife to smear the cream cheese on both. Share the butter on top of each chicken and sprinkle with salt. Wrap the bacon around the chicken and secure the ends. Place the wrapped chicken in the fryer basket and cook for 14 minutes. Turn the chicken halfway through.

Remove the chicken onto a serving platter and top with parsley and lemon juice. Serve with a side of steamed greens.

Chicken Breast with Tarragon

Total Time: 13 min | **Serves**: 2 | **Per serving**: Cal 187; Net Carbs 0.3g; Fat 5g; Protein 31g

Ingredients

2 chicken breasts, boneless and skinless
¼ cup dried tarragon

½ tbsp unsalted butter
Kosher salt and black pepper to taste

Directions

Preheat the Air Fryer to 390°F.

Place each of the chicken breasts on a foil wrap, 12x12 inches. Top the chicken with the tarragon sprig and the butter. Season with salt and pepper.

Wrap the foil around the chicken breast in a loose way, so there is a flow of air.

Cook the foil wrapped chicken in the Air Fryer for 13 minutes. Slowly and carefully unwrap the chicken and serve hot.

Crispy Chicken Schnitzel with Herbs

Total Time: 25 min | **Serves**: 2 | **Per serving**: Cal 415; Net Carbs 2.1g; Fat 34g; Protein 17g

Ingredients

2 chicken breasts, skinless and boneless
2 eggs, cracked into a bowl
2 cups coconut milk
4 tbsp tomato sauce
2 tbsp mixed herbs

2 cups mozzarella cheese
1 cup almond flour
¾ cup shaved ham
1 cup pork rinds, crushed

Directions

Place the chicken breast between to plastic wraps and use a rolling pin to pound them to flatten them out. Whisk the coconut milk and eggs together in a bowl.

Pour the flour in a plate, the pork rinds in another dish, and let's start coating the chicken.

Toss the chicken in flour, then in the egg mixture, and then in the pork rinds.

Preheat the Air Fryer to 350°F. Put the chicken in the fryer basket and cook for 10 minutes.

Remove them onto a plate and top the chicken with the ham, tomato sauce, mozzarella cheese, and mixed herbs.

Return the chicken to the fryer basket and bake further for 5 minutes or until the mozzarella cheese has melted.

Serve with a side of vegetable fries.

Garlic Chicken Tenders with Chili Aioli

Total Time: 15 min | **Serves:** 4 | **Per serving:** Cal 498; Net Carbs 2.1g; Fat 38g; Protein 41g

Ingredients

3 chicken breasts, skinless, cut into strips
4 tbsp olive oil
1 cup pork rinds, crushed
Aioli:
½ cup mayonnaise
2 tbsp lemon juice

Salt and black pepper to taste
½ tsp garlic powder
½ tsp ground chili

½ tsp ground chili

Directions

Mix pork rinds, salt, pepper, garlic powder and chili, and spread onto a plate.

Spray the chicken with oil. Roll the strips in the pork rind mixture until well coated.

Spray them with a little bit of oil. Arrange an even layer of strips into your air fryer and cook for 6 minutes at 360°F, turning once halfway through cooking.

To prepare the hot aioli: combine mayo with 2 tbsp lemon juice and ground chili.

Party Roasted Cornish Hen

Total Time: 14 hrs 26 min | **Serves**: 4 | **Per serving**: Cal 477; Net Carbs 1.2g; Fat 34.8g; Protein 37g

Ingredients

2 lb cornish hen
1 lemon, zested
¼ tsp swerve sweetener
¼ tsp salt

1 tsp fresh rosemary, chopped
1 tsp fresh thyme, chopped
¼ tsp red pepper flakes
½ cup olive oil

Directions

Place the hen on a chopping board with its back facing you and use a knife to cut through from the top of the backbone to the bottom of the spine, making 2 cuts. Remove the backbone.

Divide the hen into two lengthwise while cutting through the breastplate. Set aside.

In a bowl, add the lemon zest, swerve sweetener, salt, rosemary, thyme, red pepper flakes, and olive oil. Use a spoon to mix it well.

Add the hen pieces, coat it all around with the spoon and place it in the refrigerator to marinate for 14 hours.

Preheat the Air Fryer to 390°F.

After the marinating time, remove the hen pieces from the marinade and pat them dry using a paper towel.

Place them in the fryer basket and roast them for 16 minutes.

Remove the hen onto a serving platter and serve with veggies.

Garlic Chicken Fingers with Parmesan

Total Time: 1 hr 30 | **Serves:** 2 | **Per serving:** Cal 370; Net Carbs 2g; Fat 25g; Protein 33g

Ingredients

2 skinless chicken breasts, cut into strips
Salt and black pepper to taste
2 cloves garlic, crushed
3 tbsp xanthan gum

4 tbsp pork rinds, crushed
4 tbsp Parmesan cheese, grated
2 eggs, beaten

Directions

Mix salt, garlic, and pepper in a bowl. Add the chicken and stir to coat thoroughly. Let stay for an hour to marinate in the fridge.

Meanwhile, mix the pork rinds with cheese evenly. Set aside.

After the marinating time has passed, remove the chicken from the fridge, lightly toss in xanthan gum, dip in egg and coat them gently in the cheese mixture.

Preheat the Air Fryer to 350°F.

Lightly spray the fryer basket with cooking spray and place the chicken in it. Cook for 15 minutes. Serve the chicken with a side of vegetable fries and cheese dip. Yum!

Best Homemade Chicken Fingers

Total Time: 8 min | **Serves:** 2 | **Per serving:** Cal 132; Net Carbs 0.7g; Fat 4g; Protein 18g

Ingredients

¼ tsp fresh chives, chopped
1 tbsp Parmesan cheese, shredded
¼ tsp fresh thyme, chopped
¼ tsp black pepper

½ cup pork rinds, crushed
1 egg white
1 tsp water
5 oz chicken breast, boneless and skinless

Directions

Preheat the Air Fryer to 390°F.

Mix the chives, the Parmesan, the thyme, the pepper, and the rinds. Whisk and mix the egg white and the water. Cut the chicken breasts in large strips.

Carefully dip chicken strips into egg mixture and pork rinds mixture. Place the strips one by one in the Air Fryer basket. Cook for 8 minutes.

Sweet & Spicy Chicken Wings

Total Time: 23 min | **Serves:** 2 | **Per serving:** Cal 235; Net Carbs 1g; Fat 7g; Protein 37g

Ingredients

1 ½ tbsp hot chili sauce
½ tbsp liquid stevia
¼ tbsp the lime juice of 1 lime

12 oz chicken wings
Kosher salt and black pepper to taste

Directions

Preheat the Air Fryer to 390°F. Mix the lime juice, the stevia, and the chili sauce. Toss the chicken wings with the lime and the chili sauce mixture.

Put the chicken wings in the Air Fryer basket and cook for around 20 minutes. Shake the basket every 4 to 5 minutes. Serve hot.

Crispy Parmesan Chicken

Total Time: 33 min | **Serves**: 2 | **Per serving**: Cal 286; Net Carbs 2.3g; Fat 15g; Protein 25g

Ingredients

1 lb chicken breasts
¼ cup butter
¼ cup Parmesan cheese, grated
2 cloves garlic, minced

½ tsp dried oregano
½ tsp dried rosemary
Salt and black pepper to taste
¼ tsp paprika

Directions

Preheat the Air Fryer to 370°F.

Place the chicken in a plate and season with salt and pepper.

Put the chicken in the fryer basket, close the Air Fryer, and fry for 5 minutes.

Meanwhile, place a skillet over medium heat on a stove top, add the butter, once melted add the garlic, stir and cook it for 1 minute.

Add the paprika, oregano, and rosemary to a bowl and mix them using a spoon. Add the mixture to the butter sauce. Stir and turn off the heat.

Once the chicken breasts are ready, top them with the sauce, sprinkle with parmesan cheese and cook in the Air Fryer for 5 minutes at 360°F.

Mom's Chicken Cordon Bleu

Total Time: 35 min | **Serves:** 4 | **Per serving:** Cal 564; Net Carbs 2.2g; Fat 52g; Protein 48g

Ingredients

4 chicken breasts, skinless and boneless
4 slices Swiss cheese
4 slices ham
3 tbsp almond flour
1 tbsp paprika

4 tbsp butter
½ cup dry white wine
1 tbsp chicken bouillon granules
1 cup heavy whipping cream

Directions

Preheat the Air Fryer to 390°F.

Pound the chicken breasts and put a slice of ham on each of the chicken breasts. Fold the edges of the chicken over the filling and secure the sides with toothpicks.

In a medium bowl, combine flour and paprika and coat the chicken pieces. Set the timer to 15 minutes and cook the chicken.

In a large skillet, heat the butter and add the bouillon and the wine. Reduce the heat to low. Remove the chicken from the Air Fryer and add it to the skillet. Let the ingredients simmer for around 30 minutes and serve.

Yummy Chicken Snacks

Total Time: 25 min | **Serves:** 4 | **Per serving:** Cal 346; Net Carbs 1.6g; Fat 21g; Protein 40g

Ingredients

2 chicken breasts, cut into 2 pieces each
1 egg, beaten
¼ cup buttermilk

1 cup pork rinds, crushed
Salt and black pepper to taste

Directions

In a bowl, whisk egg and buttermilk. Add in chicken pieces and stir to coat.

In a plate, spread the pork rinds out and mix with salt and pepper. Coat the chicken pieces in the cornflakes. Spray the air fryer with oil spray.

Arrange the chicken pieces in an even layer inside your air fryer and cook for 12 minutes at 360°F, turning once halfway through cooking.

Lemon Chicken with Fresh Herbs

Total Time: 50 min | **Serves:** 5 | **Per serving:** Cal 398; Net Carbs 2.1g; Fat 28g; Protein 33g

Ingredients

2 lb chicken, cut in pieces
½ cup olive oil
3 cloves garlic, minced
1 tbsp fresh rosemary, chopped
1 tbsp fresh thyme , chopped

1 tbsp fresh oregano, chopped
2 large lemon
½ cup white wine
Salt and black pepper, to taste

Directions

In a large bowl, combine garlic, prunes, olives, capers, olive oil, vinegar, bay leaves, oregano, salt, and pepper. Mix the ingredients very well. Spread the mixture into a baking dish. Add the chicken. Keep stirring.

Preheat the Air Fryer to 350°F and place in the chicken. Sprinkle with white wine and cook it for 50 minutes.

Korean-Style Chicken

Total Time: 40 min | **Serves:** 3 | **Per serving:** Cal 243; Net Carbs 6.1g; Fat 13g; Protein 18g

Ingredients

3 cloves garlic, minced
½ lb chicken breasts, sliced
1 tbsp cumin powder
1 large onion
2 tbsp oil
1 tbsp mustard

3 green chili peppers
A pinch of ginger
A pinch of fresh coriander, chopped
2 tomatoes
Salt and black pepper, to taste

Directions

Start by heating the oil in a deep pan. Add mustard, cumin, garlic, onion, ginger, and green chili peppers. Sauté the mixture for a few minutes. Add tomatoes, coriander, cumin powder, and salt, and keep stirring.

Preheat the Air Fryer to 360°F. Coat the chicken with oil, salt, and pepper and cook it for 30 minutes. Remove from the Air Fryer and pour the sauce over and around it.

Basil & Oregano Chicken Legs

Total Time: 50 min | **Serves:** 4 | **Per serving:** Cal 483; Net Carbs 2.6g; Fat 27g; Protein 49g

Ingredients

4 quarters chicken legs
¼ cup olive oil
3 large halved lemons
4 tbsp dried oregano

4 tbsp dried basil
4 tbsp garlic powder
Salt and black pepper, to taste

Directions

Preheat the Air Fryer to 350°F.

Place the chicken legs in a deep bowl. Brush the chicken legs with a tbsp of extra virgin olive oil.

Squeeze lemon juice over the chicken and arrange in the Fryer's rack. Place the lemons around the chicken.

In a medium bowl, combine oregano, basil, garlic, salt, and pepper. Sprinkle the mixture on the chicken legs. Cook the chicken in the preheated Air Fryer for 60 minutes.

Cilantro Seed Chicken Burgers

Total Time: 25 min | **Serves:** 4 | **Per serving:** Cal 305; Net Carbs 2.3g; Fat 21g; Protein 24g

Ingredients

1 lb ground chicken
½ onion, chopped
2 garlic cloves, chopped
1 egg, beaten
½ cup pork rinds, crushed

½ tsp ground cumin
½ tsp paprika
½ tsp cilantro seeds, crushed
Salt and black pepper to taste

Directions

In a bowl, mix chicken, onion, garlic, egg, pork rinds, cumin, paprika, cilantro, salt and black.

Shape into 4 patties. Grease your air fryer oil and arrange the patties inside. Do not layer them. Cook in batches if needed. Cook for 10 minutes at 380°F, turning once halfway through cooking.

Divina's Chicken Tenders

Total Time: 15 min | **Serves:** 20 | **Per serving:** Cal 54; Net Carbs 0.2g; Fat 3g; Protein 6g

Ingredients

1.5 lb chicken tenders
20 skewers bamboo party
2 zested lemons

3 tbsp extra virgin olive oil
Salt and black pepper to taste

Directions

Preheat the Air Fryer to 350°F.

Season the chicken pieces with salt and black pepper. Thread the pieces onto skewers.

In a dish, mix lemon juice and olive oil. Coat the chicken tenders and cook the chicken tenders in the preheated Air Fryer for about 12 minutes. Serve with tomato sauce.

Party Turkey Meatballs with Parmesan

Total Time: 40 min | **Serves**: 3 | **Per serving**: Cal 245; Net Carbs 1.8g; Fat 15.7g; Protein 15.4g

Ingredients

1 lb ground turkey
1 egg
½ cup pork rinds, crushed
1 tsp garlic powder

1 tsp Italian seasoning
1 tsp onion powder
¼ cup Parmesan cheese, shredded
Salt and black pepper to taste

Directions

Preheat the Air Fryer to 400°F.

In a bowl, add the ground turkey, crack the egg onto it, add the pork rinds, garlic powder, onion powder, Italian seasoning, parmesan cheese, salt, and pepper. Mix well.

Spoon out portions and make bite-size balls out of the mixture.

Grease the fryer basket with cooking spray and add 10 turkey balls to the fryer basket.

Close the Air Fryer and cook them for 12 minutes. Slide out the fryer basket halfway through and shake it to toss the turkey.

Remove them onto a serving platter and continue the cooking process for the remaining balls. Serve the turkey balls with marinara sauce and a side of zoodles.

Green Onion & Pimento Turkey with Almonds

Total Time: 53 min | **Serves**: 3 | **Per serving**: Cal 290; Net Carbs 3g; Fat 23g; Protein 16g

Ingredients

1 lb turkey breasts
Salt and black pepper to taste
¼ cup chicken soup cream
¼ cup mayonnaise
2 tbsp lemon juice
¼ cup slivered almonds, chopped

¼ cup pork rinds, crushed
2 tbsp chopped green onion
2 tbsp chopped pimentos
2 boiled eggs, chopped
½ cup diced celery

Directions

Preheat the Air Fryer to 390°F.

Place the turkey breasts on a clean flat surface and season with salt and pepper. Grease with cooking spray and place them in the fryer basket. Close the Air Fryer and cook for 13 minutes.

Remove turkey back onto the chopping board, let cool, and use a knife to cut into dices.

In a bowl, add the celery, chopped eggs, pimentos, green onions, slivered almonds, lemon juice, mayonnaise, diced turkey, and chicken soup cream and mix well.

Grease a 3 X 3 cm casserole dish with cooking spray, scoop the turkey mixture into the bowl, sprinkle the pork rinds on it, and spray it with cooking spray. Put the dish in the fryer basket, close the Air Fryer, and bake the ingredients at 390°F for 20 minutes.

Dijon Thighs

Total Time: 30 min | **Serves**: 4 | **Per serving**: Cal 452; Net Carbs 1.2g; Fat 27g; Protein 49g

Ingredients

4 chicken thighs, skin-on
3 tbsp stevia
2 tbsp dijon mustard

½ tsp garlic powder
Salt and black pepper to taste

Directions

In a bowl, mix stevia, mustard, garlic, salt and black pepper. Coat the thighs in the mixture and arrange in your air fryer. Cook for 16 minutes at 400°F, turning once halfway through cooking.

Sweet-Soy Cauliflower with Turkey Ham

Total Time: 20 min | **Serves**: 4 | **Per serving:** Cal 123; Net Carbs 6.2g; Fat 7.5g; Protein 3.4g

Ingredients

1 big cauliflower head, cut into florets
½ cup soy sauce, sugar-free
3 tbsp stevia
1 tsp sesame oil
⅓ cup water

½ chili powder
2 cloves garlic, chopped
1 tsp psyllium husk
4 slices turkey ham, cubed

Directions

In a bowl, whisk soy sauce, stevia, sesame oil, water, chili powder, garlic and psyllium husk, until smooth.

In a separate bowl, add cauliflower, and pour teriyaki sauce over the top. Toss until well-coated. Take the cauliflower to the air fryer basket and cook for 14 minutes at 340°F, turning once halfway through cooking.

When ready, check if the cauliflower is cooked but not too soft.

Remove to a serving plate and sprinkle with turkey ham cubes to serve.

Mozzarell & Grana Padano Chicken

Total Time: 25 min | **Serves**: 2 | **Per serving:** Cal 443; Net Carbs 3.2g; Fat 25g; Protein 49g

Ingredients

2 chicken breasts, skinless, ½ inch thick
1 egg, beaten
½ cup pork rinds, crushed
A pinch of salt and black pepper

2 tbsp marinara sauce
2 tbsp Grana Padano cheese, grated
2 slices mozzarella cheese

Directions

Dip the breasts into the egg, then into the pork rinds and arrange in the air fryer. Cook for 5 minutes at 400°F.

When ready, turn over and drizzle with marinara sauce, grana padano and mozzarella cheese. Cook for 5 more minutes at 400°F.

Roasted Chicken with Pancetta & Lemon

Total Time: 60 min | **Serves:** 4 | **Per serving:** Cal 315; Net Carbs 3.6g; Fat 9.5g; Protein 52g

Ingredients

1 (3 lb) small whole chicken
1 lemon
4 slices of pancetta, chopped

1 onion, chopped
1 sprig fresh rosemary
Salt and black pepper to taste

Directions

In a bowl, mix pancetta, onion, rosemary, salt and black pepper. Pat dry the chicken with a paper towel.

Insert the pancetta mixture into chicken's cavity and press tight.

Place in the whole lemon, and rub the top and sides of the chicken with salt and black pepper.

Grease the air fryer's basket with cooking spray and put the chicken inside.

Cook for 30 minutes on 400°F, turning once halfway through cooking.

Air Fryer Chicken Nuggets

Total Time: 15 min | **Serves:** 4 | **Per serving:** Cal 311; Net Carbs 3.4g; Fat 20g; Protein 31g

Ingredients

2 chicken breasts, boneless, cut into nuggets
4 tbsp sour cream
½ cup pork rinds, crushed

½ tsp garlic powder
½ tsp cayenne pepper
Salt and black pepper to taste

Directions

In a bowl, add sour cream and place the chicken. Stir well.

Mix the pork rinds, garlic, cayenne, salt and black pepper and scatter onto a plate.

Roll up the chicken in the pork rinds to coat well.

Grease the air with cooking spray. Arrange the nuggets in an even layer and cook for 10 minutes on 360°F, turning once halfway through cooking.

Sweet Chicken Wings with Poppy Seeds

Total Time: 25 min | **Serves:** 4 | **Per serving:** Cal 215; Net Carbs 1g; Fat 11g; Protein 27g

Ingredients

1 lb chicken wings
2 tsp olive oil
2 tsp stevia
Salt and black pepper to taste
3 tbsp poppy seeds

Directions

In a bowl, add wings, oil, stevia, salt and pepper, and stir to coat well.

In another bowl, add the poppy seeds and roll the wings in the seeds to coat thoroughly.

Arrange the wings in an even layer inside your air fryer and cook for 12 minutes on 360°F, turning once halfway through cooking.

Jalapeño Peppered Chicken

Total Time: 25 min | **Serves:** 4 | **Per serving:** Cal 363; Net Carbs 3.4g; Fat 27g; Protein 26g

Ingredients

4 chicken thighs, boneless
2 garlic cloves, crushed
1 jalapeno pepper, finely chopped
4 tbsp chili sauce
Salt and black pepper to taste

Directions

In a bowl, add thighs, garlic, jalapeno, chili sauce, salt and black pepper, and stir to coat.

Arrange the thighs in an even layer inside your air fryer and cook for 12 minutes at 360°F, turning once halfway through cooking.

FISH AND SEAFOOD

Saucy Lemon Barramundi

Total Time: 25 min | **Serves**: 3 | **Per serving**: Cal 512; Net Carbs 8.1g; Fat 53g; Protein 25.3g

Ingredients

3 (½ lb) barramundi fillets
2 lemons, juiced
Salt and black pepper to taste
6 oz unsalted butter
¾ cup thickened cream

½ cup white wine
2 bay leaves
15 black peppercorns
2 cloves garlic, minced
2 shallots, chopped

Directions

Preheat the Air Fryer to 390°F.

Place the barramundi fillets on a baking paper and put them in the fryer basket. Close the Air Fryer and grill for 15 minutes. After 15 minutes, remove and put on a serving platter without the baking paper.

Place a small pan over low heat on a stove top. Add the garlic and shallots, and dry fry for a few seconds. Add the wine, bay leaves, and peppercorns. Stir and allow the liquid to reduce by three quarters. Stir in cream and let the sauce thicken into a dark cream color.

Whisk in the butter, into the cream, until fully melted. Add the lemon juice, pepper, and salt.

Turn the heat off. Strain the sauce into a serving bowl. Pour the sauce over the fish. Serve with a side of cauli rice.

Hot Catfish

Total Time: 20 min | **Serves**: 2 | **Per serving**: Cal 365; Net Carbs 5.2g; Fat 21g; Protein 33g

Ingredients

2 catfish fillets
A pinch of salt
1 cup buttermilk
2 tbsp hot sauce

2 tbsp oil for spraying
1 cup almond flour
1 tbsp crab seasoning
1 tbsp garlic powder

Directions

Season both sides of the catfish fillets with salt and pepper. In a dish, combine the buttermilk with the hot sauce.

Add the catfish fillets and cover them with sufficient liquid. Let the ingredients soak while you prepare the rest of the ingredients.

Whisk all the ingredients, almond flour, crab seasoning and garlic powder in a different casseroles. Remove the catfish from the buttermilk and let the excess oil drip off.

Now dredge the catfish on both sides with the almond flour mixture. Place 2 of the fillets in the Air Fryer basket and drizzle with oil. Set the temperature to 390°F and the time to 15 minutes.

When the cooking time is complete, open the basket, and gently turn the fillets, then spray oil and close the basket. Cook for 5 more minutes.

Balsamic Baby Octopus Salad

Total Time: 56 min | **Serves**: 3 | **Per serving**: Cal 299; Net Carbs 3.4g; Fat 20.8g; Protein 17.7g

Ingredients

1 lb baby octopus, thoroughly cleaned
1 ½ tbsp olive oil
2 cloves garlic, minced
1 ½ tbsp capers
1 ¼ tbsp balsamic glaze
1 small bunch parsley, chopped roughly
1 small bunch baby fennel, chopped

1 cup semi-dried tomatoes, chopped
1 medium red onion, sliced
2 handfuls arugula
Salt and black pepper to taste
¼ cup grilled halloumi, chopped
1 long red chili, minced
1 ½ cups water

Directions

Pour the water in a pot and bring it to boil over medium heat on a stove top.

Cut the octopus into bite sizes and add them to the boiling water for 45 seconds. Drain the water. Add the garlic, olive oil, and octopus in a bowl. Coat the octopus with the garlic and olive oil. Leave it to marinate for 20 minutes.

Preheat the Air Fryer to 390°F. Place the octopus in the basket and grill for 5 minutes.

Meanwhile, in a salad mixing bowl, add the capers, halloumi, chili, tomatoes, olives, parsley, red onion, fennel, octopus, arugula, and balsamic glaze. Season with salt and pepper and mix.

Awesome Cod Fish Nuggets

Total Time: 20 min | **Serves:** 4 | **Per serving:** Cal 168; Net Carbs 0.4g; Fat 7.5g; Protein 16.8g

Ingredients

4 cod fillets
2 tbsp olive oil
2 eggs, beaten

1 cup pork rinds, crushed
A pinch of salt
1 cup almond flour

Directions

Preheat the Air Fryer to 390°F.

Place the pork rinds, olive oil, and salt in a bowl and mix until combined. Pour the eggs into another bowl, and the almond flour into a third bowl.

Toss cod fillets in the almond flour, then in the eggs, and then in the pork rind mixture.

Place them in the fryer basket, close the Air Fryer, and cook for 9 minutes. At the 5-minute mark, quickly turn the chicken nuggets over. Once golden brown, remove onto a serving plate and serve with vegetable fries.

Rich Catfish Fillets

Total Time: 40 min | **Serves:** 2 | **Per serving:** Cal 182; Net Carbs 2.8g; Fat 12.8g; Protein 11.2g

Ingredients

2 catfish fillets
3 tbsp pork rinds, crushed
1 tsp cayenne pepper

1 tsp dry fish seasoning
2 sprigs parsley, chopped
Salt to taste

Directions

Preheat Air Fryer to 400°F.

Meanwhile, pour all the dry ingredients except the parsley in a zipper bag.

Pat dry and add the fish pieces. Close the bag and shake to coat the fish well. Do this with one fish piece at a time. Lightly spray the fish with olive oil.

Arrange them in the fryer basket, one at a time depending on the size of the fish. Close the Air Fryer and cook for 10 minutes. Flip the fish and cook further for 10 minutes.

For extra crispiness, cook further for 3 minutes. Garnish with parsley and serve.

Spicy Crab Croquettes

Total Time: 65 min | **Serves**: 6 | **Per serving**: Cal 306; Net Carbs 0.4g; Fat 15.3g; Protein 14g

Ingredients

Filling:

1 ½ lb lump crab meat

3 egg whites, beaten

⅓ cup sour cream

⅓ cup mayonnaise

1 ½ tbsp olive oil

1 red pepper, chopped finely

⅓ cup red onion, chopped

2 ½ tbsp celery, chopped

½ tsp tarragon, chopped

½ tsp chives, chopped

1 tsp parsley, chopped

1 tsp cayenne pepper

Breading:

1 ½ cup pork rinds, crushed

2 tsp olive oil

1 cup almond flour

4 eggs, beaten

Salt to taste

Directions

Place a skillet over medium heat on a stove top, add 1 ½ tbsp olive oil, red pepper, onion, and celery. Sauté for 5 minutes or until sweaty and translucent. Turn off heat.

Add the pork rinds, remaining olive oil, and salt to a food processor. Blend to mix evenly. Set aside.

In two separate bowls, add the almond flour and 4 eggs respectively. Set aside.

In a separate mixing bowl, add the crab meat, mayonnaise, egg whites, sour cream, tarragon, chives, parsley, cayenne pepper, and the celery sauté and mix evenly.

Form bite-size balls from the mixture and place into a plate.

Preheat the Air Fryer to 390°F.

Dip each crab meatball (croquettes) in the eggs mixture and press them in the pork rind mixture.

Place the croquettes in the fryer basket, 12 to 15 at a time. Avoid overcrowding. Close the Air Fryer and cook for 10 minutes or until golden brown.

Remove them and plate them. Serve the crab croquettes with tomato dipping sauce and a side of vegetable fries.

Turnip & Seafood Pie

Total Time: 60 min | **Serves**: 3 | **Per serving**: Cal 318; Net Carbs 2.7g; Fat 22.5g; Protein 24.6g

Ingredients

1 cup seafood marinara mix

1 lb turnips, peeled and quartered

1 cup water

1 carrot, grated

½ head baby fennel, grated

1 bunch dill sprigs, chopped

1 sprig parsley, chopped

A handful of baby spinach

1 small tomato, diced

½ celery sticks, grated

2 tbsp butter

1 tbsp coconut milk

½ cup grated cheddar cheese

1 small red chili, minced

½ lemon, juiced

Salt and black pepper to taste

Directions

Pour the turnips into a pan, add the water, and bring it to a boil over medium heat on a stove top. Use a fork to check that it is soft and mash-able, after about 12 minutes. Drain the water and use a potato masher to mash it.

Add butter, coconut milk, salt, and pepper. Mash until smooth and well mixed. Set aside.

In a bowl, add the celery, carrots, cheese, chili, fennel, parsley, lemon juice, seafood mix, dill, tomato, spinach, salt, and pepper. Mix well. Preheat the Air Fryer to 330°F.

In a 15 cm casserole dish, add half of the carrots mixture and level it. Top with half of the turnip mixture and level it.

Place the dish in the Air Fryer and bake for 20 minutes ensuring that the mash is golden brown and the seafood is cooked properly.

Remove the dish and add the remaining seafood mixture and level it out. Top with the remaining turnip mash and level it too. Place the dish back into the Air Fryer and cook at 330°F for 20 more minutes. Once ready, remove the dish. Slice the pie and serve.

Jumbo Prawn in Bacon Rolls

Total Time: 32 min | **Serves**: 3 | **Per serving**: Cal 133; Net Carbs 0.1g; Fat 12.1g; Protein 13.6g

Ingredients

8 bacon slices

8 Jumbo prawns, peeled and deveined

Lemon wedges for garnishing

Directions

Wrap each prawn from head to tail with each bacon slice overlapping to keep the bacon in place.

Secure the end of the bacon with a toothpick. It's ok not to cover the ends of the cheese with bacon. Refrigerate for 15 minutes.

Preheat the Air Fryer to 400°F.

Arrange the bacon wrapped prawns in the fryer's basket.

Close the Air Fryer and cook for 7 minutes or until the bacon has browned and crispy. Transfer prawns to a paper towel to cool for 2 minutes.

Remove the toothpicks and serve the bacon wrapped prawns with lemon wedges.

Perfect Salmon Quiche

Total Time: 8 min | **Serves:** 4 | **Per serving:** Cal 515; Net Carbs 2.6g; Fat 54g; Protein 11g

Ingredients

5 oz salmon fillet, cubed
2 cups almond flour
1 cup cold butter, cubed
4 tbsp whipping cream

2 large eggs and 1 yolk
1 large green onion, finely sliced
1 tbsp lemon juice
A pinch of black pepper

Directions

Preheat the Air Fryer to 360°F., if needed.

Season salmon fillets with salt, pepper and lemon juice. Set it aside.

In a large bowl, stir in the butter.

Add the egg yolk, 1 tbsp of water and knead the entire mixture into one ball. Roll the dough onto a floured hard surface.

Put the round dough into the quiche pan and seal on the edges.

Trim the dough to fit the edges of the pan you intend to use or just let it stick out. Beat eggs with cream, then add a pinch of salt and pepper.

Pour the mixture into the quiche pan, and add the green onions.

Slide the quiche pan in the Air Fryer's basket and set the timer to 20 minutes and the heat to 350°F.

Easy Coconut Shrimp

Total Time: 15 min | **Serves:** 4 | **Per serving:** Cal 156; Net Carbs 3.2g; Fat 2g; Protein 17g

Ingredients

½ cup water
½ tbsp baking powder
1 tbsp salt
½ cup almond flour
½ tbsp red pepper flakes

4 tbsp rice wine vinegar
½ cup strawberry marmalade
2 cups shredded sweetened coconut
½ cup pork rinds, crushed
1 lb large shrimp, peeled and deveined

Directions

For the dipping sauce: add red pepper flakes, vinegar, and marmalade to a saucepan. Heat around 10 minutes on low heat. Keep stirring until the mixture is combined.

Now, in a deep bowl, whisk the salt, the flour, and the baking powder. Add water. Whisk everything until the mixture becomes smooth. Set the batter aside for 15 minutes.

In another bowl, toss the coconut and pork rinds. Dip each shrimp into batter and then coat it with coconut mixture. Set the heat to 390°F and fry them for 3 minutes. Serve the shrimp with the dipping sauce.

Dilled Salmon

Total Time: 25 min | **Serves:** 4 | **Per serving:** Cal 240; Net Carbs 0g; Fat 6g; Protein 16g

Ingredients

4 (6-oz) salmon pieces
Salt and black pepper to taste
2 tsp olive oil

3 tbsp chopped dill + extra for garnishing
1 cup sour cream
1 cup Greek yogurt

Directions

Make the dill sauce: in a bowl, add the sour cream, yogurt, dill, and salt. Mix it well.

Preheat the Air Fryer to 270°F.

Drizzle the olive oil over the salmon. Season with salt and pepper. Rub lightly with your hands. Arrange the salmon pieces in the fryer basket and cook them for 15 minutes.

Remove the salmon onto the serving platter and top with dill sauce. Serve with steamed asparagus.

Paprika-Rubbed Jumbo Shrimp

Total Time: 15 min | **Serves**: 3 | **Per serving**: Cal 112; Net Carbs 1g; Fat 5g; Protein 15g

Ingredients

1 lb jumbo shrimp
Salt to taste
¼ tsp old bay seasoning

⅓ tsp smoked paprika
¼ tsp cayenne pepper
1 tbsp olive oil

Directions

Preheat the Air Fryer to 390°F.

In a bowl, add the shrimp, paprika, oil, salt, old bay seasoning, and cayenne pepper. Combine well.

Place the shrimp in the fryer basket, close the Air Fryer, and cook for 5 minutes.

Remove the shrimp onto a serving plate.

Fennel Trout en Papillote with Herbs

Total Time: 30 min | **Serves**: 2 | **Per serving**: Cal 305; Net Carbs 8.9g; Fat 21.1g; Protein 9.6g

Ingredients

¾ lb whole trout, scaled and cleaned
¼ bulb fennel, sliced
½ brown onion, sliced
3 tbsp chopped parsley

3 tbsp chopped dill
2 tbsp olive oil
1 lemon, sliced
Salt and black pepper to taste

Directions

In a bowl, add the onion, parsley, dill, fennel, and garlic. Mix and drizzle the olive oil over it.

Preheat the Air Fryer to 350°F.

Open the cavity of the fish and fill with the fennel mixture. Wrap the fish thoroughly in parchment paper and then in foil. Place the fish in the fryer basket and cook for 10 minutes.

Remove the paper and foil and top with lemon slices. Serve with a side of cooked mushrooms.

Simple Pomfret Fish Fry

Total Time: 15 min | **Serves:** 5 | **Per serving:** Cal 463; Net Carbs 3.4g; Fat 23g; Protein 55g

Ingredients

3 lb silver pomfret
1 tbsp turmeric powder
3 pinches of red chili powder
¾ tbsp ginger

3 pinches of cumin powder
2 tbsp lemon juice
2 tbsp olive oil
Salt and black pepper, to taste

Directions

Wash the fish and soak in lemon juice to remove any unpleasant smell.

After 30 minutes, remove and wash the fish. Draw diagonal shaped slits on the fish. Combine black pepper, salt, garlic paste, lemon juice, and the turmeric powder.

Rub the mixture above and inside the fish and refrigerate for 30 minutes.

Arrange the fish in the basket of the Air Fryer and pour 2 tbsp of oil. Cook it for 12 minutes at 340°F.

Herb Crusted Halibut

Total Time: 30 min | **Serves:** 4 | **Per serving:** Cal 287; Net Carbs 1.3g; Fat 18g; Protein 22g

Ingredients

¾ cup pork rinds, crushed
4 halibut fillets
½ cup fresh parsley, chopped
¼ cup fresh dill, chopped

¼ cup fresh chives, chopped
1 tbsp extra virgin olive oil
1 tbsp finely grated lemon zest
Sea salt and black pepper to taste

Directions

Preheat the Air Fryer to 390°F.

In a large bowl, mix the pork rinds, the parsley, the dill, the chives, the olive oil, the lemon zest, the sea salt, and black pepper.

Rinse the halibut fillets and dry them on a paper towel. Arrange the halibut fillets on a baking sheet.

Spoon the rinds on the fish. Lightly press the crumb mixture on the fillet. Cook the fillets in a preheated Air Fryer's basket for 30 minutes.

Fried Spinach Fish

Total Time: 10 min | **Serves:** 2 | **Per serving:** Cal 173; Net Carbs 0.5g; Fat 18g; Protein 4g

Ingredients

4 oz spinach leaves
2 cups almond flour
A pinch of salt

2 tbsp oil
1 large beaten egg

Directions

In a deep bowl, add beaten egg, wheat flour, salt, and spinach leaves. Marinate the fish. Cook in the Air Fryer for 12 minutes at 370°F. Serve with lemon slices.

Easy Bacon Wrapped Shrimp

Total Time: 15 min | **Serves:** 4 | **Per serving:** Cal 95; Net Carbs 3.2g; Fat 7g; Protein 6g

Ingredients

2 pounds king shrimp
16 bacon strips, cooked

Barbecue sauce, to serve

Directions

Wrap the shrimp with bacon strips, then secure with toothpicks. Cook at 390°F for 5 minutes. Shake the basket from time to time. Serve the shrimp with the BBQ sauce.

Mediterranean Halibut

Total Time: 35 min | **Serves:** 6 | **Per serving:** Cal 432; Net Carbs 7.1g; Fat 32g; Protein 27g

Ingredients

2 lb halibut fillets, cut in 6 pieces
Salt and black pepper
3-4 chopped green onions

½ cup mayonnaise
½ cup sour cream
1 tbsp dried dill weed

Directions

Preheat the Air Fryer to 390°F. Season the halibut with salt and pepper.

In a bowl, mix onions, mayonnaise, sour cream, and dill. Spread this mixture over the fish. Cook for 20 minutes.

Lemon-Zest Salmon

Total Time: 20 min | **Serves:** 2 | **Per serving:** Cal 421; Net Carbs 1.3g; Fat 17g; Protein 64g

Ingredients

2 salmon fillets
Pink salt to taste

Zest of 1 lemon

Directions

Spray the fillets with cooking spray. Rub them with salt and lemon zest.

Line baking paper in your air fryer's basket to avoid sticking. Cook the fillets for 10 minutes at 360°F, turning once halfway through cooking. Serve with steamed asparagus and a drizzle of lemon juice.

Crispy Fish Strips

Total Time: 20 min | **Serves:** 4 | **Per serving:** Cal 183; Net Carbs 2.6g; Fat 6.7g; Protein 24g

Ingredients

2 fresh white fish fillets, cut into 4 fingers each
1 egg, beaten
½ cup buttermilk

1 cup pork rinds, crushed
Salt and black pepper to taste

Directions

In a bowl, mix egg and buttermilk. On a plate, mix pork rinds, salt and black pepper.

Dip each finger into the egg mixture, then roll it up in the pork rinds, and grease with cooking spray. Arrange them in the air fryer and cook for 10 minutes at 340°F, turning once halfway through cooking. Serve with garlic mayo and lemon wedges.

Garlic & Chili Prawns

Total Time: 12 min | **Serves:** 1 | **Per serving:** Cal 151; Net Carbs 3.2g; Fat 2g; Protein 23g

Ingredients

8 prawns, cleaned
Salt and black pepper to taste
½ tsp ground cayenne pepper

½ tsp chili flakes
½ tsp ground cumin
½ tsp garlic powder

Directions

In a bowl, season the prawns with salt and black pepper. Sprinkle cayenne, flakes, cumin and garlic and stir to coat. Grease the air fryer's basket and arrange the prawns in an even layer. Cook for 8 minutes at 340°F, turning once halfway through cooking.

Chinese Fish with Mushrooms

Total Time: 12 min | **Serves**: 4 | **Per serving:** Cal 267; Net Carbs 3.5g; Fat 8g; Protein 39g

Ingredients

2 lb white fish fillets
½ tbsp salt
4 mushrooms, sliced
1 tbsp liquid stevia
2 onions, sliced

4 tbsp soy sauce
2 tbsp red chili powder
2 tbsp vinegar
2 tbsp Chinese winter pickle

Directions

Fill the fish with the pickle and mushrooms. Spread the onion on the fish. In a bowl, combine the vinegar, soy sauce, stevia, and salt. Sprinkle over the fish, and cook in the Fryer for 10 minutes at 350°F.

Restaurant-Style Dragon Shrimp

Total Time: 10 min | **Serves**: 2 | **Per serving:** Cal 405; Net Carbs 5.2g; Fat 27g; Protein 31g

Ingredients

½ lb shrimp
½ cup soy sauce
2 eggs
2 tbsp olive oil

1 cup onions, chopped
A pinch of ginger, grated
¼ cup almond flour

Directions

Boil the shrimps for around 5 minutes.

Prepare a paste made of ginger and onion. Beat the eggs and add ginger, onion, soya sauce, almond flour and mix them very well. Add shrimps to the mixture and cook them for 10 minutes, at 390°F. Remove from the Air Fryer and serve with keto mayo.

Ginger Cedar Planked Salmon

Total Time: 35 min | **Serves:** 6 | **Per serving:** Cal 476; Net Carbs 4.1g; Fat 38g; Protein 33g

Ingredients

4 untreated cedar planks
½ cup vegetable oil
1½ tbsp rice vinegar
1 tbsp sesame oil
½ cup soy sauce

¼ cup green onions, chopped
1 tbsp fresh ginger root, grated
1 tbsp garlic, grated
2 lb salmon fillets, skin removed

Directions

Start by soaking the cedar planks for 2 hours.

Take a shallow dish and stir in the vegetable oil, the rice vinegar, the sesame oil, the soy sauce, the green onions, and ginger. Put the salmon fillets in the prepared marinade for at least 20 minutes.

Place the planks in the basket of the Air Fryer. Cook for 15 minutes at 360°F.

Delicious Octopus with Green Chilies

Total Time: 35 min | **Serves:** 3 | **Per serving:** Cal 195; Net Carbs 4.2g; Fat 7g; Protein 25g

Ingredients

3 roots coriander, washed
7 medium green chilies
2 cloves garlic
A pinch of salt
2 drops liquid stevia

2 small limes
1 tbsp olive oil
1 lb clean octopus
1 tsp fish sauce

Directions

Mash the washed roots of coriander in the mortar.

Add the green chilies, the 2 cloves of garlic, a pinch of salt, stevia, 1 teaspoon of fish sauce, the juice of 2 limes and a teaspoon of olive oil. Put the dipping sauce in a bowl. Cut the octopus into tentacles.

Arrange the tentacles of the octopus in the Air Fryer basket and set the heat to 370°F. Cook them for 4 minutes on each side. Serve with the dipping sauce.

Quick Tuna Sandwich with Mozzarella

Total Time: 10 min | **Serves:** 2 | **Per serving:** Cal 451; Net Carbs 7.2g; Fat 17g; Protein 61g

Ingredients

4 slices zero carb bread
2 small tins of tuna, drained
½ onion, finely chopped

2 tbsp mayonnaise
1 cup mozzarella cheese, shredded

Directions

Lay your zero carb bread out onto a board.

In a small bowl, mix tuna, onion, mayonnaise. Spoon the mixture over 2 bread slices.

Top with cheese and put the other piece of bread on top.

Spray with cooking spray each side and arrange the sandwiches into the air fryer.

Cook at 360°F for 6 minutes, turning once halfway through cooking.

Hot Crab Cakes with Green Onions

Total Time: 20 min | **Serves:** 8 | **Per serving:** Cal 121; Net Carbs 1.5g; Fat 5.5g; Protein 14g

Ingredients

1 lb crab meat, shredded
2 eggs, beaten
½ cup pork rinds, crushed
⅓ cup green onions, chopped
¼ cup parsley, chopped

1 tbsp mayonnaise
1 tsp chili sauce
½ tsp paprika
Salt and black pepper to taste

Directions

In a bowl, add meat, eggs, pork rinds, green onion, parsley, mayo, chili sauce, paprika, salt and black pepper and mix well with hands.

Shape into 8 cakes and grease them lightly with cooking spray.

Arrange the cakes into the fryer, without overcrowding. Cook for 8 minutes at 400°F, turning once halfway through cooking.

Mixed Seafood with Yogurt

Total Time: 15 min | **Serves:** 4 | **Per serving:** Cal 211; Net Carbs 5.2g; Fat 8.1g; Protein 24g

Ingredients

1 lb of mixed seafood
2 eggs, lightly beaten
Salt and black pepper to taste

1 cup pork rinds, crushed mixed with the zest of 1 lemon
Yogurt, for dipping

Directions

Clean the seafood as needed. Dip each piece into the egg. Season with salt and pepper.

Coat in the pork rinds and spray with oil. Arrange into your air fryer and cook for 6 minutes at 400°F, turning once halfway through cooking.

Pork Rind & Almond-Coated Scallops

Total Time: 5 min | **Serves:** 6 | **Per serving:** Cal 105; Net Carbs 2.7g; Fat 3.4g; Protein 14g

Ingredients

12 fresh scallops
3 tbsp almond flour
Salt and black pepper to taste

1 egg, lightly beaten
1 cup pork rinds, crushed

Directions

Coat the scallops with almond flour. Dip into the egg, then into the pork rinds. Spray them with cooking spray and arrange them in the air.

Cook for 6 minutes at 360°F, turning once halfway through cooking.

Lime Salmon with Broccoli

Total Time: 25 min | **Serves:** 2 | **Per serving:** Cal 511; Net Carbs 7.2g; Fat 21g; Protein 64g

Ingredients

2 salmon fillets
1 tsp olive oil
Juice of 1 lime
1 tsp chili flakes

Salt and black pepper to taste
1 head of broccoli, cut into florets
1 tsp olive oil
1 tbsp soy sauce, sugar-free

Directions

In a bowl, add oil, lime juice, flakes, salt and black pepper.

Rub the mixture onto fillets. Lay the florets into your air fryer and drizzle with oil. Arrange the fillets around or on top and cook for 10 minutes at 340°F.

Drizzle the florets with soy sauce to serve.

Crispy Fish & Turnip Chips

Total Time: 25 min | **Serves**: 4 | **Per serving:** Cal 265; Net Carbs 3.3g; Fat 10.3g; Protein 34g

Ingredients

2 turnips, cut into thin slices chips
Salt and black pepper to taste
4 white fish fillets
2 tbsp almond flour
1 egg, beaten
1 cup pork rinds, crushed
Salt and black pepper to taste

Directions

Grease the turnip chips with cooking spray and season with salt and black pepper.

Places them in the air fryer, and cook for 20 minutes at 400°F.

Meanwhile, spread almond flour on a plate and coat the fish.

Dip them in the egg, then into the pork rinds and season with salt and black pepper.

At the 10 minutes' mark, add the fish to the fryer and cook with the chips.

Cook until crispy. Serve with lemon slices.

MEATLESS RECIPES

Basil Tofu

Total Time: 30 min | **Serves**: 2 | **Per serving**: Cal 187; Net Carbs 4.3g; Fat 14.4g; Protein 10g

Ingredients

6 oz extra firm tofu

Black pepper to taste

1 tbsp vegetable broth

1 tbsp soy sauce, sugar-free

⅓ tsp dried oregano

⅓ tsp garlic powder

⅓ tsp dried basil

⅓ tsp onion powder

Directions

Place the tofu on a cutting board. Cut it into 3 lengthwise slices with a knife.

Line a side of the cutting board with paper towels, place the tofu on it and cover with a paper towel.

Use your hands to press the tofu gently until as much liquid has been extracted from it. Remove the paper towels and use a knife to chop the tofu into 8 cubes. Set aside.

In another bowl, add the soy sauce, vegetable broth, oregano, basil, garlic powder, onion powder, and black pepper. Mix well with a spoon.

Pour the spice mixture on the tofu, stir the tofu until well coated, and place it aside to marinate for 10 minutes. Preheat the Air Fryer to 390°F.

Arrange the tofu in the fryer basket in a single layer. Cook the tofu for 6 minutes.

Slide out the fryer basket and turn the tofu using a spatula.

Slide it back in and continue cooking for 4 minutes. Remove onto a plate and serve with a side of green salad.

Pine Nuts & Roasted Brussels Sprouts

Total Time: 20 min | **Serves:** 6 | **Per serving:** Cal 112; Net Carbs 5.4g; Fat 7.4g; Protein 7g

Ingredients

15 oz Brussels sprouts, cut in half

1 tbsp olive oil

Salt to taste

1 ¾ oz pine nuts, toasted

Directions

In a large bowl, pop the sprouts with oil and salt and stir to combine well.

Preheat your Air Fryer to 390°F. Add the sprouts to the Air Fryer cooking basket and roast for 15 minutes; check often.

Remove Brussel sprouts from the air fryer and mix with toasted pine nuts.

Curry Mixed Veggie Bites

Total Time: 2 hrs | **Serves**: 16 bites | **Per serving**: Cal 160; Net Carbs 2g; Fat 8g; Protein 3g

Ingredients

1 medium cauliflower, cut in florets
6 medium carrots, diced
1 medium broccoli, cut in florets
½ cup cauli rice, not steamed
1 onion, diced
½ cup garden peas
2 leeks, sliced thinly
1 small courgette, chopped
⅓ cup almond flour

1 tbsp garlic paste
2 tbsp olive oil
1 tbsp curry paste
2 tsp mixed spice
1 tsp coriander
1 tsp cumin powder
1 ½ cups coconut milk
1 tsp ginger paste
Salt and black pepper to taste

Directions

Steam all the vegetables except the leek and courgette for 10 minutes. Set aside.

Place a wok over medium heat; add the onion, ginger, garlic and olive oil. Stir-fry until onions turn transparent. Add the leek, courgette and curry paste. Stir and cook for 5 minutes.

Add all the listed spices, coconut milk, and cauli rice. Stir and simmer for 10 minutes.

Once the sauce has reduced, add the steamed veggies. Mix evenly. Transfer into a bowl and refrigerate for 1 hour.

Remove the veggie base from the fridge and mold into bite sizes. Arrange the veggie bites in the fryer basket and close the Air Fryer. Cook at 350°F for 10 minutes.

Once they are ready, it is time to serve them.

Serve with yogurt dipping sauce for the best taste.

Double Cheese Vegetable Frittata

Total Time: 35 min | **Serves**: 2 | **Per serving**: Cal 380; Net Carbs 8.4g; Fat 28.3g; Protein 24g

Ingredients

1 cup baby spinach
⅓ cup mushrooms, sliced
1 large zucchini, sliced
1 small red onion, sliced
¼ cup chives, chopped
¼ lb asparagus, trimmed and sliced

2 tsp olive oil
4 eggs, cracked into a bowl
⅓ cup almond milk
Salt and black pepper to taste
⅓ cup cheddar cheese, grated
⅓ cup feta cheese, crumbled

Directions

Preheat the Air Fryer to 320°F. Line a 3 X 3 baking dish with parchment paper. Set aside.

In the egg bowl, add the almond milk, salt, and pepper. Beat evenly.

Place a skillet over medium heat on a stove top, add olive oil.

Once heated, add the asparagus, zucchini, onion, mushrooms, and baby spinach. Sauté for 5 minutes while stirring.

Pour the sautéed veggies into the baking dish and pour the egg mixture over.

Sprinkle the feta and cheddar cheese over it and place it in the Air Fryer. Close the Air Fryer and cook it for 15 minutes.

Once ready, remove the baking dish and garnish with the fresh chives.

Mixed Vegetables with Sesame Dipping Sauce

Total Time: 20 min | **Serves**: 8 | **Per serving**: Cal 96; Net Carbs 5.6g; Fat 5.1g; Protein 3.1g

Ingredients

2 lb chopped mixed veggies
1 ½ cups almond flour
Salt and black pepper to taste

1 ½ tbsp chia seeds
¾ cup cold water

Dipping sauce:

4 tbsp soy sauce, sugar-free
Juice of 1 lemon
½ tsp sesame oil
½ tsp sugar

½ garlic clove, chopped
½ tsp chili sauce

Directions

Line the air fryer basket with baking paper.

In a bowl, mix almond flour, salt, pepper, and chia seeds and whisk to combine. Keep whisking as you add water into the dry ingredients to a smooth batter is formed.

Dip each veggie piece into the batter and place into your air fryer. Cook for 12 minutes at 360°F, turning once halfway through cooking. Cook them until crispy.

For the dipping sauce, mix all ingredients in a bowl.

Bell Peppers Filled with Cauli Rice and Cheese

Total Time: 40 min | **Serves**: 4 | **Per serving**: Cal 215; Net Carbs 5.4g; Fat 16g; Protein 13g

Ingredients

4 bell peppers
Salt and black pepper to taste
½ cup olive oil
1 red onion, chopped
1 large tomato, chopped

½ cup goat cheese, crumbled
3 cups cauli rice
2 tbsp Parmesan cheese, grated
2 tbsp fresh basil, chopped
1 tbsp lemon zest

Directions

Preheat the Air Fryer to 350°F.

Cut the peppers a quarter way from the head down and lengthwise. Remove the membrane and seeds. Season the peppers with black pepper and salt, and drizzle olive oil over.

Place the pepper bottoms in the fryer basket and cook them for 5 minutes at 350°F to soften a little.

In a mixing bowl, add the tomatoes, goat cheese, lemon zest, basil, and cauli rice. Season with salt and pepper. Mix well.

Remove the Pepper bottoms from the Air Fryer onto a flat surface and spoon the cheese mixture into them.

Sprinkle parmesan cheese on top of each and gently place in the fryer basket.

Bake for 15 minutes. Remove once ready onto a serving platter.

Chili Brussels Sprouts with Garlic Aioli

Total Time: 25 min | **Serves**: 4 | **Per serving**: Cal 52; Net Carbs 2.1g; Fat 2.6g; Protein 5.1g

Ingredients

1 lb Brussels sprouts, trimmed
Salt and black pepper to taste
1 ½ tbsp olive oil
2 tsp lemon juice

1 tsp powdered chili
3 cloves garlic
¾ cup mayonnaise
2 cups water

Directions

Place a skillet over medium heat on a stove top, add the garlic cloves with the peels on it and roast until lightly brown and fragrant.

Remove the skillet with the garlic and place a pot with water over the same heat. Bring it to a boil.

Using a knife, cut the brussels sprouts in halves lengthwise. Add to the boiling water to blanch for just 3 minutes. Drain through a sieve and set aside.

Preheat the Air Fryer to 350°F.

Remove the garlic from the skillet to a plate; peel and crush and set aside. Add olive oil to the skillet and light the fire to medium heat on the stove top. Stir in the brussels sprouts, season with pepper and salt. Sauté for 2 minutes. Turn off the heat. Pour the brussels sprouts in the fryer basket and bake for 5 minutes.

Meanwhile, make the garlic aioli. In a bowl, add the mayonnaise, crushed garlic, lemon juice, powdered chili, pepper and salt in a bowl. Mix well.

Remove the brussels sprouts onto a serving bowl and serve with the garlic aioli.

Mediterranean Sandwiches with Pesto

Total Time: 60 min | **Serves**: 2 | **Per serving**: Cal 541; Net Carbs 8.3g; Fat 49g; Protein 16.2g

Ingredients

1 heirloom tomato, sliced
1 (4-oz) block feta cheese, sliced
1 small red onion, thinly sliced
1 clove garlic
Salt to taste

2 tsp + ¼ cup olive oil
1 ½ tbsp pine nuts, toasted
¼ cup parsley, chopped
¼ cup Parmesan cheese, grated
¼ cup basil, chopped

Directions

Start with the pesto: Add the basil, pine nuts, garlic and salt to the food processor. Process it while adding the ¼ cup of olive oil slowly.

Once the oil is finished, pour the basil pesto into a bowl and refrigerate it for 30 minutes

Preheat the Air Fryer to 390°F.

Remove the pesto from the fridge and use a tablespoon to spread some pesto on each slice of tomato. Top with a slice of feta cheese.

Add the onion and remaining olive oil in a bowl and toss. Spoon on top of the feta cheese on the tomato. Carefully place the tomato in the fryer basket, close the air fryer, and bake it for 12 minutes.

Remove the tomatoes to a plate, sprinkle with salt and top with any remaining pesto.

Homemade Assorted Chips

Total Time: 50 min | **Serves**: 4 | **Per serving**: Cal 120; Net Carbs 6g; Fat 3.5g; Protein 3g

Ingredients

1 large eggplant
5 medium parsnips
3 medium zucchinis
½ cup arrowroot starch
½ cup water
½ cup olive oil
Salt to taste

Directions

Preheat the Air Fryer to 390°F. Cut the eggplant and zucchini in long 3-inch strips. Peel the parsnips and cut them in 3-inch strips. Place aside.

In a bowl, add the arrowroot starch, water, salt, pepper, olive oil, eggplants, zucchini, and parsnips and stir well to combine.

Place one-third of the veggie strips in the fryer basket, close the Air Fryer and cook them for 12 minutes. Once ready, transfer them to a serving platter.

Repeat the cooking process for the remaining veggie strips until they are all done. Serve warm as a side to a meat dish or with spicy or sweet sauce.

Quick Fall Vegetable Delight

Total Time: 31 min | **Serves**: 3 | **Per serving**: Cal 77; Net Carbs 3g; Fat 3g; Protein 2g

Ingredients

1 small parsnip, sliced in a 2-inch thickness
1 cup butternut squash, chopped
2 small red onions, cut in wedges
1 cup celery, chopped

1 tbsp fresh thyme, chopped
Salt and black pepper to taste
2 tsp olive oil

Directions

Preheat the Air Fryer to 200 F.

In a bowl, add the parsnips, butternut squash, red onions, celery, thyme, pepper, salt, and olive oil and mix well.

Pour the vegetables into the fryer basket, close the Air Fryer, and cook for 16 minutes. Transfer the roasted veggies into a serving bowl.

Zucchini & Turnip Bake

Total Time: 30 min | **Serves**: 3 | **Per serving**: Cal 55; Net Carbs 2.4g; Fat 4.9g; Protein 1g

Ingredients

3 turnips, sliced
1 large red onion, cut into rings
1 large zucchini, sliced
Salt and black pepper to taste

2 cloves garlic, crushed
1 bay leaf, cut in 6 pieces
1 tbsp olive oil

Directions

Place the turnips, onion, and zucchini in a bowl. Toss with olive oil and season with salt and pepper.

Preheat the Air Fryer to 330°F.

Place the veggies into a baking pan that fits in the Air Fryer. Slip the bay leaves in the different parts of the slices and tuck the garlic cloves in between the slices. Insert the pan in the Air Fryer basket and cook for 15 minutes.

Once ready, remove and serve warm with as a side to a meat dish or salad.

Cauliflower Florets with Pine Nuts

Total Time: 34 min | **Serves**: 4 | **Per serving**: Cal 140; Net Carbs 1g; Fat 7g; Protein 5g

Ingredients

1 large cauliflower head, cut into florets
Salt to taste
1 ½ tbsp curry powder

½ cup olive oil
⅓ cup pine nuts, toasted

Directions

Preheat the Air Fryer to 390°F. Add the pine nuts and 1 teaspoon of olive oil in a medium bowl. Mix with the tablespoon.

Pour them in the fryer basket and cook them for 2 minutes. Remove them into a bowl to cool. Place the cauliflower in a large mixing bowl. Add the curry powder, salt, and the remaining olive oil and mix well.

Transfer to the fryer basket in 2 batches and cook each batch for 10 minutes.

Remove the curried florets onto a serving platter, sprinkle with the pine nuts, and toss. Serve the florets with a tomato sauce or a side to a meat dish.

Parsley & Cheese Stuffed Mushrooms

Total Time: 9 min | **Serves**: 4 | **Per serving**: Cal 117; Net Carbs 0.9g; Fat 11g; Protein 2.7g

Ingredients

14 small button mushrooms
1 clove garlic, minced
Salt and black pepper to taste

¼ cup cheddar cheese, grated
1 tbsp olive oil
1 tbsp parsley, chopped

Directions

Preheat the Air Fryer to 390°F. In a bowl, add the olive oil, cheddar cheese, parsley, salt, pepper, and garlic. Mix them well using a spoon.

Cut the stalks of the mushroom off and fill each cap with the bacon mixture.

Press the cheese mixture into the caps to avoid any from falling off.

Place the stuffed mushrooms in the fryer basket, close the Air Fryer and cook at 390°F for 8 minutes. Once golden and crispy, remove them onto a serving platter. Serve with green salad.

Keto Sushi with Cauli Rice

Total Time: 60 min | **Serves:** 4 | **Per serving:** Cal 178; Net Carbs 5.8g; Fat 15g; Protein 2.4g

Ingredients

2 cups cauli rice

4 nori sheets

1 carrot, sliced lengthways

1 red bell pepper, seeds removed, sliced

1 avocado, sliced

1 tbsp olive oil

1 tbsp wine vinegar

1 cup almonds, crushed

2 tbsp sesame seeds

Wasabi and pickled ginger to serve

Directions

Prepare a clean working board, a small bowl of lukewarm water and a sushi mat.

Wet hands, and lay a nori sheet onto a sushi mat and spread half cup cauli rice, leaving a half inch of nori clear, so you can seal the roll.

Place the carrot, bell pepper and avocado sideways to the cauli rice. Roll tightly the sushi and rub warm water along the clean nori strip to seal them.

In a bowl, mix olive oil and vinegar. In another bowl, mix the crushed almonds with the sesame seeds. Roll each sushi log in the vinegar mixture and then straight to the sesame bowl to coat.

Arrange the coated sushi into the air fryer and cook for 14 minutes at 360°F, turning once halfway through cooking.

When ready, check if the sushi is golden and crispy on the outside. Slice and serve with pickled ginger and wasabi.

Sage Parsnip & Cheese Bake

Total Time: 30 min | **Serves:** 8 | **Per serving:** Cal 131; Net Carbs 5.6g; Fat 8.3g; Protein 6.7g

Ingredients

3 tbsp pine nuts

28 oz parsnips, chopped

1 ¾ oz Parmesan cheese, chopped

6 ¾ oz crème fraiche

1 slice zero carbs bread

2 tbsp dried sage

4 tbsp butter

4 tsp mustard

Directions

Preheat your Air Fryer to 360°F.

Boil parsnips in salted water in a pot over medium heat. Drain and mash them with butter using a potato masher.

In a mixing bowl, mix mustard, crème fraiche, sage, salt and pepper. Add parsnip mash, zero carb bread, cheese, and nuts and mix. Cook in your Air Fryer for 25 minutes.

Balsamic Glazed Beets

Total Time: 20 min | **Serves**: 2 | **Per serving:** Cal 75; Net Carbs 7.5g; Fat 4.1g; Protein 3.6g

Ingredients

4 beets, cubed
⅓ cup balsamic vinegar
1 tbsp olive oil

4 drops liquid stevia
Salt and black pepper to taste
2 sprigs rosemary, chopped

Directions

In a mixing bowl, mix rosemary, pepper, salt, vinegar and stevia. Cover beets with the prepared sauce and then coat with oil.

Preheat your Air Fryer to 400°F. Place the beets in the Air Fryer cooking basket and cook for 10 minutes. Pour the balsamic vinegar in a pan over medium heat; bring it to a boil and cook until reduced by half. Drizzle the beets with balsamic glaze to serve.

Balsamic Parsnips & Zucchini

Total Time: 30 min | **Serves**: 8 | **Per serving:** Cal 143; Net Carbs 6.5g; Fat 5g; Protein 2g

Ingredients

2 lb chopped veggies: parsnips and zucchini
3 tbsp olive oil
1 tbsp balsamic vinegar

1 tbsp stevia
2 garlic cloves, minced
Salt and black pepper to taste

Directions

In a bowl, add oil, balsamic vinegar, stevia, garlic, salt and black pepper. Mix well with a fork. Arrange the veggies into the fryer, drizzle with the dressing and massage with hands until well-coated. Cook for 25 minutes at 360°F, tossing halfway through cooking.

The Best Zucchini Fries

Total Time: 25 min | **Serves:** 4 | **Per serving:** Cal 367; Net Carbs 5g; Fat 28g; Protein 11g

Ingredients

3 medium zucchini, sliced
2 egg whites
½ cup seasoned pork rinds, crushed

2 tbsp Parmesan cheese, grated
¼ tsp garlic powder
Salt and black pepper to taste

Directions

Preheat your Air Fryer to 425°F. Coat cooling rack with cooking spray and place in your air fryer's cooking basket.

In a mixing bowl, beat the egg whites and season with salt and pepper. In another bowl, mix garlic powder, cheese and pork rinds.

Take zucchini slices and dredge them in eggs, followed by pork rinds. Add zucchini to the rack and spray more oil. cook for 20 minutes. Serve and enjoy!

Tasty Rosemary Squash

Total Time: 30 min | **Serves:** 2 | **Per serving:** Cal 68; Net Carbs 4.6g; Fat 0.2g; Protein 2.3g

Ingredients

1 butternut squash
1 tbsp dried rosemary
Salt to taste

Directions

Place the butternut squash on a cutting board and peel it. Cut it in half and remove the seeds. Cut the pulp into wedges and season with salt.

Preheat the Air Fryer to 350°F.

Spray the squash wedges with cooking spray and sprinkle the rosemary on it.

Grease the fryer basket with cooking spray and place the wedges in it without overlapping.

Slide the fryer basket back in and cook for 10 minutes.

Flip the wedges and cook further for 10 minutes. Serve right away with a dip.

Amasing Veggie Halloumi

Total Time: 15 min | **Serves**: 2 | **Per serving:** Cal 420; Net Carbs 8.2g; Fat 26g; Protein 22g

Ingredients

6 oz block of firm halloumi cheese, cubed
2 zucchinis, cut into even chunks
1 large carrot, cut into chunks
1 large eggplant, peeled, cut into chunks
2 tsp olive oil
1 tsp dried mixed herbs
Salt and black pepper to taste

Directions

In a bowl, add halloumi, zucchini, carrot, eggplant, olive oil, herbs, salt and pepper. Sprinkle with oil, salt and pepper.

Arrange halloumi and veggies in the air fryer and cook for 14 minutes at 340°F.

When ready, make sure the veggies are tender and the halloumi is golden.

Sprinkle with olive oil and scatter with fresh arugula leaves.

DESSERTS

Chocolate Topped Meringue Cookies

Total Time: 45 min | **Serves:** 4 | **Per serving:** Cal 45; Net Carbs 6.4g; Fat 0.5g; Protein 7.6g

Ingredients

8 egg whites
½ tsp almond extract
1 ⅓ cup granulated stevia
¼ tsp salt

2 tsp lemon juice
1 ½ tsp vanilla extract
Melted dark chocolate to drizzle

Directions

In a mixing bowl, add the egg whites, salt, and lemon juice. Beat using an electric mixer until foamy.

Slowly add the stevia and continue beating until thoroughly combined.

Add the almond and vanilla extracts. Beat until stiff peaks form and glossy. Line a round baking sheet with parchment paper, that fits into the fryer basket.

Fill a piping bag with the meringue mixture and pipe as many mounds on the baking sheet as you can leaving 2-inch spaces between each mound.

Place the baking sheet in the fryer basket and bake at 350°F for 5 minutes.

Reduce the temperature to 320°F and bake for 15 more minutes. The, reduce the heat once more to 290 F and cook for 15 minutes.

Remove the baking sheet and let the meringues cool for about 2 hours. Drizzle with the dark chocolate before serving.

Dark Chocolate and Peanut Butter Fondants

Total Time: 25 min | **Serves:** 4 | **Per serving:** Cal 316; Net Carbs 8.1g; Fat 22g; Protein 9.5g

Ingredients

¾ cup dark chocolate
½ cup Peanut butter, crunchy
2 tbsp butter, diced
¼ cup + ¼ cup swerve sugar

4 eggs, room temperature
1/8 cup almond flour, sieved
1 tsp salt
¼ cup water

Directions

Make a salted praline to top the chocolate fondant. Add ¼ cup of sugar, 1 tsp of salt and the water into a saucepan. Stir and bring it to a boil over low heat on a stove top. Simmer until the desired color is achieved and reduced. Pour into a baking tray and leave it to cool and harden.

Preheat the Air Fryer to 300°F.

Place a pot of water over medium heat and place a heatproof bowl over it. Add the chocolate, butter, and peanut butter to the bowl. Stir continuously until fully melted, combined, and smooth.

Remove the bowl from the heat and allow it to cool slightly. Add the eggs to the chocolate and whisk it. Add the flour and remaining sugar and mix well.

Grease 4 small loaf pans with cooking spray and divide the chocolate mixture between them. Place the pans, 2 pans at a time in the fryer basket and bake for 7 minutes.

Easy Lemon Curd

Total Time: 32 min | **Serves**: 2 | **Per serving**: Cal 260; Net Carbs 1g; Fat 16g; Protein 12g

Ingredients

3 tbsp butter
3 tbsp swerve sugar
1 egg
1 egg yolk
¾ lemon, juiced

Directions

Add the sugar and butter in a medium ramekin and use a hand mixer to beat evenly. Add the egg and yolk slowly while still whisking. Add the lemon juice and mix it.

Place the bowl in the fryer basket and start cooking at 170°F for 3 minutes.

Then, increase the temperature to 190 F and cook for 3 minutes. Increase the heat again to 210°F and cook for 6 minutes, then 230°F for 6 minutes, and finally to 250°F for 6 minutes.

Remove the bowl onto a flat surface. Use a spoon to check for any lumps and remove.

Cover the ramekin with a plastic wrap and refrigerate it overnight or serve immediately.

Vanilla Chocolate Souffle

Total Time: 40 min | **Serves**: 2 | **Per serving**: Cal 320; Net Carbs 3.1g; Fat 25g; Protein 11g

Ingredients

3 oz unsweetened chocolate

4 large egg whites

2 large egg yolks, at room temperature

¼ cup erythritol + more for garnishing

1 tbsp butter, melted

1 tbsp butter, unmelted

¼ tsp vanilla extract

1 ½ tbsp almond flour

Directions

Coat 2 6-oz ramekins with melted butter.

Add the erythritol and swirl it in the ramekins to coat the butter. Pour out the remaining sugar and keep it.

Melt the unmelted butter with the chocolate in a microwave and set aside.

In another bowl, beat the egg yolks vigorously. Add the vanilla and kept sugar. Beat to incorporate fully. Add the chocolate mixture and mix well. Add the almond flour and mix it with no lumps.

Preheat the Air Fryer to 330°F.

Whisk egg whites in another bowl until it holds stiff peaks. Add ⅓ of the egg whites to the chocolate mixture and fold in gently.

Share the mixture into the ramekins with ½ inch space left at the top. Place the ramekins in the fryer basket and cook for 14 minutes. Dust with the remaining erythritol and serve.

Raspberry & Chocolate Cake

Total Time: 40 min | **Serves**: 8 | **Per serving**: Cal 317; Net Carbs 9.2g; Fat 24g; Protein 6g

Ingredients

1 ½ cups almond flour

⅓ cup cocoa powder

2 tsp baking powder

¾ cup white sugar

¼ cup stevia

¾ cup butter

2 tsp vanilla extract

1 cup almond milk

1 tsp baking soda

2 eggs

1 cup freeze-dried raspberries

1 cup dark chocolate chips, unsweetened

Directions

Line a cake tin with baking powder.

In a bowl, mix almond flour, cocoa and baking powder.

Place the stevia, butter, vanilla, almond milk and baking soda into a microwave-safe bowl and heat for 60 seconds until the butter has melted and the ingredients incorporate. Let cool slightly.

Whisk the eggs into the mixture. Pour the wet ingredients into the dry ones, and fold to combine.

Add in the raspberries and chocolate chips. Pour the batter into the tin and cook for 30 minutes at 350°F.

Air Fryer Crème Brulee

Total Time: 70 min | **Serves**: 3 | **Per serving**: Cal 409; Net Carbs 3.5g; Fat 32.5g; Protein 8.5g

Ingredients

1 cup whipped cream
1 cup coconut milk
2 vanilla pods
10 egg yolks
4 tbsp swerve sugar + extra for topping

Directions

In a pan, add the coconut milk and cream. Cut the vanilla pods open and scrape the seeds into the pan with the vanilla pods also.

Place the pan over medium heat on a stove top until almost boiled while stirring regularly. Turn off the heart. Add the egg yolks to a bowl and beat it. Add the sugar and mix well but not too frothy.

Remove the vanilla pods from the coconut milk mixture and pour the mixture onto the eggs mixture while stirring constantly. Let it sit for 25 minutes. Fill 2 to 3 ramekins with the mixture.

Place the ramekins in the fryer basket and cook them at 250°F for 50 minutes.

Once ready, remove the ramekins and let sit to cool. Sprinkle the remaining swerve sugar over and use a torch to melt the sugar, so it browns at the top.

Quick Breton Butter Cake

Total Time: 20 min | **Serves:** 8 | **Per serving:** Cal 287; Net Carbs 0.8g; Fat 31g; Protein 4g

Ingredients

1 cup butter
¼ cup liquid stevia
1 tbsp pure vanilla extract
6 egg yolks

3 cups almond flour
¼ tsp salt
1 large egg, lightly beaten

Directions

Preheat the Air Fryer to 350°F.

In the bowl of an electric mixer, combine cream butter and stevia. Keep mixing until it becomes fluffy. Add vanilla and yolk gradually, and beat well after each yolk.

Now, transfer the batter into a 9-inch pan, with removable bottom. Smooth the surface with a spatula.

Chill the batter in the fridge before baking it for 15 minutes. Then brush it with a beaten egg and cook in the Fryer for 35 minutes.

Mom's Lemon Cake

Total Time: 40 min | **Serves:** 16 | **Per serving:** Cal 231; Net Carbs 0.1g; Fat 27g; Protein 1.5g

Ingredients

2 cups warm butter
¼ cup liquid stevia
A pinch of salt
4 large eggs
1 grated and untreated lemon rind
2 cups almond flour
2 tbsp baking powder

Directions

Line a baking pan with a parchment paper. Beat the warm butter, the stevia, and the salt.

Add eggs and lemon zest; beat until the mixture becomes creamy and consistent. Sift in the flour and the baking powder. Pour the batter into the baking pan. Cook at 320°F for 35 minutes.

Awesome Coconut Cups

Total Time: 15 min | **Serves:** 8 | **Per serving:** Cal 75; Net Carbs 0.6g; Fat 7g; Protein 1.3g

Ingredients

1 cup almond flour
1 tbsp baking powder
1 large egg
1 tbsp liquid stevia
¾ cup coconut milk

Directions

In a bowl, mix the flour and the baking powder. In a separate bowl, beat eggs and stevia until thick. Add in the egg and coconut milk until all combined.

Take a baking pan and line ramekins inside it.

Pour the batter evenly into the ramekins, making sure the poured mixture is thin. Cook the ramekins for 3 minutes at 325°F. Serve the pikelets with butter.

Easy Coconut Flour Bread

Total Time: 40 min | **Serves:** 6 | **Per serving:** Cal 215; Net Carbs 0.6g; Fat 22g; Protein 6.5g

Ingredients

6 medium eggs
½ tbsp erythritol
½ cup coconut oil
¾ cup coconut flour
1 tbsp baking powder

Directions

Preheat the Air Fryer to 360°F. In a deep bowl, sift coconut flour, and add baking powder. Set aside.

In a separate bowl, mix the eggs, oil, erythritol and a pinch of salt. Add the dry ingredients and mix well.

Spoon the batter into a greased loaf baking pan. Cook in the Air Fryer for 35 minutes.

Blueberry Sandwiches with Chocolate

Total Time: 30 min | **Serves:** 2 | **Per serving:** Cal 256; Net Carbs 9.6g; Fat 15g; Protein 14g

Ingredients

4 slices zero carb bread
1 tbsp butter, melted
6 oz dark chocolate, broken into chunks
1 cup blueberries

Directions

Brush the zero carb bread slices with butter. Spread chocolate and blueberries on 2 bread slices. Top with the remaining 2 slices to create 2 sandwiches.

Arrange the sandwiches into your air fryer and cook for 14 minutes at 400°F, turning once halfway through cooking. Slice in half and serve.

Cinnamon Baked Granny Smith Apples

Total Time: 35 min | **Serves:** 2 | **Per serving:** Cal 283; Net Carbs 10.2g; Fat 20.5g; Protein 4g

Ingredients

2 Granny Smith apples, cored, bottom intact
2 tbsp butter, cold
3 tbsp stevia
3 tbsp crushed walnuts
1 tsp cinnamon

Directions

In a bowl, add butter, stevia, walnuts, and cinnamon and mix with fingers until you obtain a crumble. Arrange the apples in the air fryer.

Stuff them with the filling mixture. Cook for 30 minutes at 400°F.

Air Fryer Sponge Cake

Total Time: 45 min | **Serves:** 12 | **Per serving:** Cal 183; Net Carbs 0.5g; Fat 21g; Protein 1.7g

INGREDIENTES:

1 cup butter
½ cup liquid stevia
4 large eggs
2 cups almond flour

Directions

Preheat the Air Fryer to 350°F. Grease and flour a jelly roll pan.

In a deep bowl, cream butter and stevia until the mixture becomes light and soft. Beat in eggs, adding them one by one.

Sift in almond flour and keep mixing until the batter becomes smooth. Spread the dough in the baking pan. Cook in the Air Fryer 350°F for 40 minutes.

Vanilla Rolled Cookies

Total Time: 10 min + chilling time | **Serves:** 8 | **Per serving:** Cal 341; Net Carbs 0.5g; Fat 35g; Protein 3g

Ingredients

1 ½ cups butter, softened
4 tbsp liquid stevia
4 large eggs
1 tbsp vanilla extract
4 cups almond flour
2 tbsp baking powder

Directions

In a deep bowl, cream the butter and the stevia until smooth. Beat in the eggs and the vanilla. Add in flour, baking powder and 1 tsp of salt.

Cover the mixture and let chill for 2 hours. Preheat the Air Fryer to 390°F. Roll out the dough on a floured surface. Cut the dough into cookies shapes. Arrange them in the basket and cook for 10 minutes.

CONCLUSION

Going keto has been one of the best things that happened to me and with the use of very available ingredients to cook makes life so much easier.

Now, with the air fryer, I never get tired of trying new things, tweaking the ingredients and my previous recipes here and there. The results are endless, and you will find a lot of joy in making these dishes.

A quick piece of advice before I sign off, always use fresh vegetables, fat trimmed meats, and reduced sugar sauces. The best drink to take on a diet like this is WATER which will aid the digestion process faster and easier.

Made in the USA
Middletown, DE
13 June 2019